THE OBSERVER'S
POCKET SERIES

. . .

THE OBSERVER'S BOOK
OF SHIPS

The Observer's Books

THE OBSERVER'S BOOK OF

SHIPS

By

FRANK E. DODMAN

Foreword by
A. C. HARDY, B.Sc., M.I.N.A., F.R.G.S.

Describing over
ONE HUNDRED TYPES
with 95 line drawings,
16 colour plates
and 16 plates of photographs

FREDERICK WARNE & CO. LTD.
LONDON AND NEW YORK

Copyright
FREDERICK WARNE & CO. LTD.
LONDON

First published 1952
New edition 1958

Printed in Great Britain

PREFACE

SINCE the first edition of this book was published in 1952 there have been important developments in the world of shipping.

A different conception of the function and composition of a navy, new methods of propulsion, and the introduction of guided missiles are altering the appearance of warships. Battleships are no longer required. The dominant part played by heavy long-range guns has been taken by the carrier-borne aircraft; these in turn may be replaced by guided missiles fired from nuclear submarines. The conventional forms of smaller warships also are giving way to new and unfamiliar lines.

The *Southern Cross* was the first large passenger vessel to be built with engines aft. Other larger liners are now under construction with similar silhouettes. Inevitably nuclear power will change the appearance of the merchant ship to some extent.

The Russian icebreaker *Lenin* and the United States submarine *Nautilus* have led the way with the new revolutionary form of propulsion; but a nuclear-powered aircraft carrier is projected and more submarines, tankers and at least one passenger liner should be on the stocks by the end of the year. These are all expensive prototypes of the ships of the future.

The new edition contains new and revised text and many new line drawings; most of the plates have been replaced by fresh material. Some alterations have been made in the plates of flags and funnels and a key, which classifies the companies under funnel colours, has been added to facilitate reference "in the field." My thanks are

5

due to the shipping companies which have supplied the necessary information.

I am particularly grateful to those companies which have lent colour transparencies and other colour material for reproduction. Their kindness is hereby acknowledged.

Thanks are also due to the French Naval Attaché in London and to the Admiralty for photographs of warships, and to the Controller, H.M. Stationery Office, for his permission to reproduce the flags and a selection of signals from the International Code of Signals.

Finally, I should like to thank those who have made useful criticisms and whose suggestions have been incorporated, as far as possible, in the second and subsequent editions.

Poole, Dorset   FRANK E. DODMAN

CONTENTS

COLOUR PLATES

HALF-TONE PLATES

(The line drawings and unacknowledged photographs are by the author).

8

FOREWORD

To design a ship is a complicated business. To design a book about ships hardly less so. All ship design is a compromise between the various requirements of departments in a ship-owning organization, each with individualistic ideas. Designing a book for the observers of ships must be a truly gigantic task, when you think as I do as President of the World Ship Society of the number of ship lovers there are, each with his own individual love.

When Frank Dodman produced his original book in 1952 he made it of a size which would slip into a pocket; and there is nothing that a ship lover likes more than to wander around docks or harbours and see his favourites moving in and out, and to note with approval or disapproval the recent alterations which have been made in their shape, appearance and colours.

It is a happy privilege to be able to follow the late W. J. Bassett-Lowke in providing a foreword to this book. Few people had a greater zest for ships than he, and few did more to interest the general public.

Ships are the greatest fun in the world, and they bring a vast amount of pleasure to a number of people. The *Observer's Book of Ships*, as a collection of factual data alone, is more than worth the money you pay for it. This is its twelfth edition, and I feel sure that it is going to have a long and successful life.

A. C. HARDY

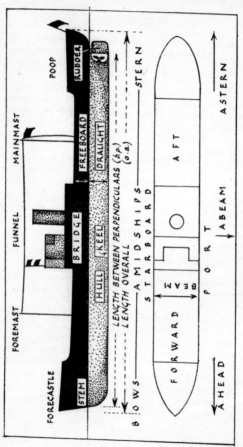

FIG. 1.—Nautical terms

GLOSSARY OF NAUTICAL TERMS

MANY other terms are described or illustrated on Figs. 1 and 2, and on the drawings showing the parts of a merchant ship, warship, sailing ship, yacht, and fishing vessel.

ATHWARTSHIPS. From one side of the ship to another—across the ship.

BALLAST. Sand, gravel, or water carried by a ship when she is without cargo, to keep her propeller sufficiently submerged. Most vessels are fitted with water tanks and pumps specially for this purpose. Iron or lead weights placed in a yacht's bottom to counterbalance the heel when sailing.

BILGE. The curve of a hull where it changes from the side to the bottom. Some vessels have bilge keels to prevent rolling.

BULWARK. Steel or wooden wall round the ship's sides, giving protection to the deck.

CABLE. Approximately one-tenth of a nautical mile, or 200 yds.

CAMBER. The athwartships curve of a ship's deck. Exactly like the camber of a roadway.

COMPANION. Staircase or ladder down a hatchway. A ladder which can be lowered at ship's side to give access to water or quay level from deck.

DAVITS. Small cranes or apparatus for lifting and lowering ship's lifeboats. The oldest and simplest type is a pair of curved steel pillars. Later types have patent mechanical devices for speedier and more efficient lowering.

DOCKING BRIDGE. A platform at the stern for an officer to assist in controlling the ship's movements during docking operations. Usually connected by telegraph to the navigating bridge.

FLARE. The upward curve of the ship's side at the bows.

GOALPOST MAST. Twin masts or sampson posts with a cross bar.

HATCHWAY. Opening in the deck through which cargo is loaded, or any opening giving access to space below decks. Steamers' hatchways are covered by hatch-boards, beams, and tarpaulins. The small boat's hatchway is covered by a sliding hatch.

KNOT. A nautical mile per hour.

NAUTICAL MILE. 6,080 ft. One minute of latitude at the Equator.

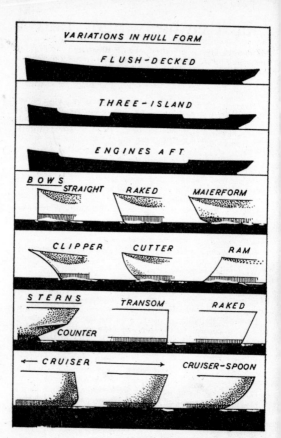

FIG. 2.—Variations in hull form

PLIMSOLL OR LOAD LINE. Marks painted on the sides of a merchant ship to indicate the safe depth to which she may be loaded (see drawing). The Ministry of Transport is responsible for the load-line regulations for British ships.

QUARTER. The ship's sides near the stern.

SHEER. The fore-and-aft curve of a ship's decks, rising towards the bows and stern. A warship's deck usually rises towards the bows only.

STRAKE. A horizontal line of plating or planking on the ship's sides. A rubbing strake is a permanent hard-wooded band along the ship's sides to protect the plating from chafing against quays and piers: a characteristic feature of the coaster and cross-Channel ship.

TRIM. The way the ship "sits" in the water, i.e. on an even keel, down by the head, or down by the stern.

TRUCK. Round piece of wood at the top of a mast.

WEATHER DECK. Uppermost deck of the hull—not superstructure.

WELL DECK. Deck space between either forecastle and bridge or bridge and poop.

Some abbreviations·

S.S.	Steamship	D/F	Direction Finder
M.V.	Motor Vessel	W/T	Wireless Telephony or Wireless Telegraphy
M.S.	Motor Ship		
S.Y.	Steam Yacht	A.B.	Able-bodied seaman
T.S.	Turbine Steamer or Training ship	H.M.S.	Her Majesty's Ship
		R.I.N.	Royal Indian Navy
R.M.S.	Royal Mail Steamer	R.P.N.	Royal Pakistan Navy
R.Y.S.	Royal Yacht Squadron	R.A.N.	Royal Australian Navy
M.N.	Merchant Navy	R.C.N.	Royal Canadian Navy
F.V.	Fishing Vessel	R.N.	Royal Navy
T.S.S.	Twin Screw Steamer	R.N.L.I.	Royal National Lifeboat Institution
o.a.	Length overall		
b.p.	Length between perpendiculars	R.N.R.	Royal Naval Reserve
		R.N.V.R.	Royal Naval Volunteer Reserve
g.t.	Gross register tonnage		

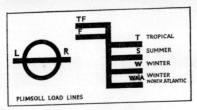

FIG. 3.—Plimsoll load lines

13

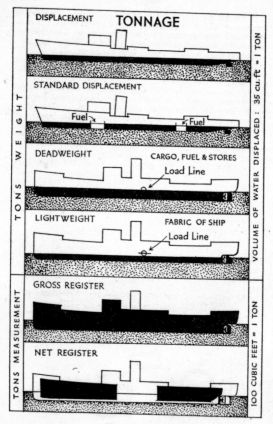

FIG. 4.—Tonnage

TONNAGE

SHIP tonnage sometimes confuses the layman, particularly when he finds that one ship can have five different figures, the highest often three times larger than the lowest. A medium-sized freighter could have the tonnage figures 10,000, 7,500, 3,000, 5,200, and 3,500, and the diagrams opposite show, in a very much simplified way, how the different tonnages are calculated. Any comparison between tonnage figures must obviously refer to the same sort of tonnage for each of the ships concerned.

It is important to distinguish between the two kinds of "tons": one is weight avoirdupois and the other is equivalent to 100 cu. ft. of enclosed space. With regard to merchant ships, *gross*, *net*, and *deadweight* tonnage figures are normally used. There is no hard-and-fast relationship between these figures, and unless ships are of the same type with the same functions comparisons are likely to be misleading. For example:

Type	Gross	Net	Deadweight
Freighter . .	5,000	3,000	7,000
Tanker . .	6,700	4,000	10,000
Passenger Liner .	20,000	12,000	10,000

DISPLACEMENT TONNAGE. This represents the total weight of the ship and everything on board. The volume of water displaced varies a little according to whether the water is salt, fresh, or in particular parts of the world. This tonnage is not used for merchant ships but always for warships. Since 1920 standard displacement has been the official figure, that is, the full displacement less the weight of fuel and reserve feed water. All warship tonnages given in this book are standard displacement.

DEADWEIGHT (dwt.). This is the weight in tons avoirdupois (or 20 cwt.) of the cargo, stores, fuel, etc., carried by a merchant ship when down to her loading marks (Plimsoll line, see page 13). It is equal to loaded displacement less the weight of the ship, the latter being the lightweight tonnage. The deadweight tonnage of a ship is a good indication of her cargo-carrying and earning capacity.

GROSS REGISTER (g.t.). The total cubic capacity of all enclosed space at 100 cu. ft. to the ton. Used for general purposes and in national maritime registers.

NET REGISTER. Measured in the same way as gross tonnage, the net register is the capacity of enclosed space *less* that of the engine and boiler rooms, crew accommodation, stores, and all spaces necessary for the working of the ship. In other words, it is the cubic capacity of all earning space, and it is on this tonnage figure that most harbour dues and other charges are calculated.

METHODS OF MECHANICAL PROPULSION

STEAM RECIPROCATING ENGINES. The first passenger steamship was the *Comet* of 1812. She was propelled by a simple four-horse-power engine driving at first two, and later one pair of paddles. Fuel consumption was large and consequently her trips were short. All early steamships suffered from the handicap of excessive fuel consumption. The simple engine developed into the two-cylinder compound engine and eventually became the triple-expansion compound engine as we know it to-day. The steam, generated in Scotch fire-tube boilers, passes successively through a small high-pressure cylinder, a medium-pressure and a large low-pressure cylinder. The triple-expansion engine is slow but economical and reliable.

STEAM REACTION TURBINES. Acting on a principle similar to that of the water wheel, the steam—generated in water-tube boilers—passes through numerous fine nozzles on to small blades fixed round the rim of a cylinder, thus forcing it to revolve. The average turbine revolves at a speed of about 4,000 r.p.m. and before this power can be transmitted to the propeller shaft the rotational speed must be reduced through single or double reduction gearing to a speed of about 100 r.p.m. This mechanically simple type of engine is efficient, quiet, and smooth-running, and it is particularly suitable for fast passenger liners although it is used for some fast cargo liners, cross-Channel packets, and most warships.

ELECTRIC PROPULSION. In electrically-driven ships the shafts are connected up to electric motors for which the power is generated by either diesel- or steam-turbine-driven generators. Turbo-electric machinery is often employed for large ocean-going tankers, for a small number of passenger liners, and a number of tugs (page 105). The latest British trawlers are driven in this way (*see* page 143).

DIESEL MOTORS. The general principle of the marine motor engine is similar to that of the motor-car internal-combustion engine except that the oil fuel is ignited by compression. Compared with the steam engine the fuel consumption is much lower. An added advantage is the fact that fuel is not consumed when the ship is lying in port. Each year diesels are fitted to an increasing number of ships from 100-ton coasters up to 25,000-ton liners.

GAS TURBINES. In 1947 a British gunboat was fitted with gas turbines for sea-going tests and early in 1952 the British tanker *Auris* (12,000 tons dwt.) was driven across the Atlantic by an experimental gas turbine fitted in addition to diesel-electric machinery. She has now been re-engined with a single 5,500-h.p. gas turbine. The American freighter *John Sergeant* was the first pure gas-turbine merchant vessel. Some British fast Patrol Boats (*see* page 99) are powered by gas turbines, and a new type of propulsion machinery, combining gas turbines with steam turbines, is now in use in fast escort vessels and some freighters.

NUCLEAR REACTORS. This latest form of marine propulsion is based on the use of nuclear fuel which, in minute bulk, can give a tremendous cruising range. The first atomic ship was the U.S. submarine *Nautilus* which completed a voyage of 50,000 miles without re-fuelling. Similar submarines are under construction, and the first British nuclear-powered ship will be the submarine *Dreadnought*. Many difficulties have to be faced before this form of power can be an economical proposition for the merchant ship, but plans for giant nuclear-powered tankers are already in preparation.

FIG. 5.—BUOYAGE SYSTEM OF THE UNITED KINGDOM

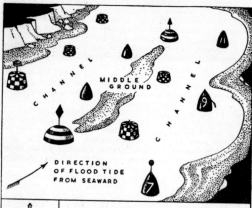

CHANNEL

MIDDLE GROUND

CHANNEL

DIRECTION OF FLOOD TIDE FROM SEAWARD

Starboard-hand buoys are conical in shape and painted in a single colour. They mark the *right*-hand side of a channel entering from seaward and the *left*-hand when proceeding seawards.

Port-hand buoys are *can* or *barrel* shaped and are either parti-coloured or a single colour different from the starboard buoys. They mark the *left*-hand side of a channel entering from seaward and the *right*-hand when proceeding seawards.

Middle Ground buoys are spherical in shape and painted in horizontal white and coloured stripes. They mark sandbanks or shoals in the middle of a channel or division between two channels.

Wreck buoys are painted green with WRECK in large white letters. They may be conical, can or spherical shaped according to which side a vessel may safely pass.

Fig. 6.—NAVIGATION LIGHTS FOR VESSELS OVER 150 FT. IN LENGTH

Anchor or Riding Lights. An all-round white light on the forestay 20 ft. to 40 ft. above the hull and at the stern a similar white light 15 ft. lower than the forward light.

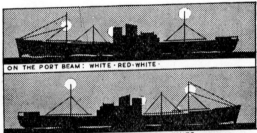

ON THE PORT BEAM: WHITE·RED·WHITE·

ON THE STARBOARD BEAM: WHITE·GREEN·WHITE

FROM STARBOARD BOW: RIGHT AHEAD FROM PORT BOW

Steaming Lights. A white light on the foremast 20 ft. to 40 ft. above the hull visible ahead and two points (22½°) abaft either beam; a similar white light on the mainmast at least 15 ft. higher than the forward light. *Side or Bow Lights,* placed lower than the white lights and visible right ahead and two points abaft the beam, *red* on the *port* side and *green* on the *starboard* side. A white *stern light* is shown by a vessel when being overtaken.

INTERNATIONAL CODE

(*See* Plate I)

THE present version of the International Code of Signals came into being in 1934 and is used by all nations at all times. The Royal Navy has its own code, although many of the same flags are used.

SIGNAL LETTERS

Besides the letter values shown in Plate I, each flag has a signal value. For example, the letter **D** also means "keep clear of me—I am manœuvring with difficulty." Every ship and even many small yachts have a four-letter identification signal. British ships have either **G** or **M** as the first letter. The letter **F** represents France, **PA** or **PI** Holland, and **K, N,** or **W** the United States of America.

Every phrase likely to be used at sea is represented by a group of code letters. Each ship carries the official International Code books which contain all these recognized signals. If it is necessary to send an unusual signal, perhaps containing someone's name, the words may be spelt out letter by letter. To economize in flags, substitute flags are used; for instance, in the signal indicating the port of Plymouth **A M P M** the last letter would be indicated by the second substitute flag instead of repeating the letter **M**.

Signals flags should always be flown from a point where they can be read without obstruction from masts or stays. If more than one point is used the signal reads from forward aft.

On festive occasions in port, ships of all types may "dress ship," that is, fly all the code flags on a taut line hoisted from the stem or bowsprit over the trucks of the masts down to the stern.

In the Royal Navy code flags are arranged in a prescribed order; other ships have no ruling for dressing ship, but for the sake of uniformity they can use a standard arrangement devised by the Admiralty.

SIGNAL FLAGS: SELECTION OF SIGNALS

SINGLE-LETTER SIGNALS

A I am undergoing a speed trial. **B** I am taking in or discharging explosives. **C** Yes (Affirmative). **D** Keep clear of me—I am manœuvring with difficulty. **E** I am altering my course to starboard. **F** I am disabled. Communicate with me. **G** I require a pilot. **H** I have a pilot on board. **I** I am altering my course to port. **J** I am going to send a message by semaphore. **K** You should stop your vessel instantly. **L** You should stop. **I** have something important to communicate. **M** I have a doctor on board. **N** No (Negative). **O** Man overboard. **P** (Blue Peter). *In harbour:* All persons are to repair on board as the vessel is about to proceed to sea. (Flown at foremast.) *At sea:* Your lights are out or burning badly. **Q** My vessel is healthy, I request a free pratique. **R** The way is off my ship; you may feel your way past me. **S** My engines are going full speed astern. **T** Do not pass ahead of me. **U** You are standing into danger. **V** I require assistance. **W** I require medical assistance. **X** Stop carrying out your intentions and watch for my signals. **Y** I am carrying mails. **Z** To be used to address or call all shore stations.

A SELECTION OF TWO-LETTER SIGNALS

A M Accident has occurred, I require a doctor. **N C** I am in distress and require immediate assistance, **S C** What is the name of your vessel?

SELECTION OF THREE-LETTER SIGNALS

E C E What course are you steering? **P Y U** Good voyage.

FOUR-LETTER SIGNALS

Ports. **A A A S** Aberdeen. **A J J O** Liverpool. **A G J V** Glasgow.

Ships. **G B T T** *Queen Mary.* **P G G F** *Nieuw Amsterdam.* **G R S X** *Strathaird.* **G Y K S** *Caronia* **G S W Q** *Parthia.*

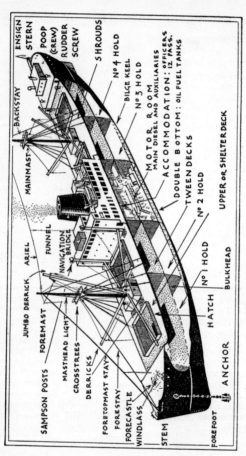

FIG. 7.—Parts of a cargo vessel

SAMPSON POSTS
FORMAST
MASTHEAD LIGHT
CROSSTREES
DERRICKS
FORETOPMAST STAY
FORESTAY
FORECASTLE
WINDLASS
STEM
FOREFOOT
ANCHOR

JUMBO DERRICK
ARIEL
FUNNEL
NAVIGATION BRIDGE
MAINMAST
BACKSTAY

ENSIGN
STERN
POOP (CREW)
RUDDER
SCREW
SHROUDS
Nº 4 HOLD
BILGE KEEL
Nº 3 HOLD
MOTOR ROOM
MAIN DIESEL AND AUXILIARIES
ACCOMMODATION: OFFICERS.
12 PASS.
OIL FUEL TANKS
DOUBLE BOTTOM:
TWEEN DECKS
Nº 2 HOLD
UPPER OR SHELTER DECK
BULKHEAD
HATCH
Nº 1 HOLD

MERCHANT SHIPS

PARTS OF A CARGO VESSEL

THE hull of a typical cargo-carrier is a flat-bottomed steel structure divided into a number of water-tight compartments by vertical steel walls called transverse bulkheads. These bulkheads separate the holds from the machinery space. The double bottom consists of an inner and outer skin with tanks between for oil fuel and water ballast. The machinery space of the motor ship takes up much less room than that of the average steamship with her engine room, boilers, and coal fuel bunkers. The holds are divided horizontally by one or two decks with hatchways giving access to the lower holds. The passenger liner may have several decks and as many as fifteen transverse bulkheads. The *Queens* (*see* page 31) also have an inner and outer skin, several feet apart, on each side of the midship section of the hull.

The drawing—Fig. 7—shows a flush-decked vessel with a raised forecastle and raised poop and a compact bridge superstructure which comprises the navigating bridge, boat deck, passengers' and officers' accommodation. The crew (rarely berthed in the forecastle) are accommodated in the poop. The derricks are capable of lifting three- to five-ton loads and many vessels are fitted with a jumbo derrick for weights of about twenty tons. Each derrick is equipped with a steam or electric winch. The hatchways are covered by movable steel hatch-beams and wooden hatch-boards finally sealed with tarpaulins securely wedged along the hatch-coamings; many modern ships are equipped with labour-saving steel hinged hatches (*see* page 47). The conventional mast, with rigging of stays and shrouds, is now giving way to the self-supporting bipod mast (*see* Fig. 71 and Plate VI) which requires no obstruction and little maintainance.

FIG. 8.—Comparative silhouettes of merchant ships—I

24

COMPARATIVE SILHOUETTES

(Fig. 8)

No.	Type	Gross Register Tonnage	Length overall in feet	Breadth in feet	Draught in feet	Speed in knots	Date of Building	Propulsion	Page
a	TRANSATLANTIC PASSENGER AND MAIL LINER	83,000	1,031	119	39	28	1940	T	31
b	PASSENGER LINER	22,200	658	78	31	20	1926	T	33
c	FRUIT CARRIER	3,600	354	47	21	15	1934	M	59
d	PASSENGER AND CARGO LINER	10,000	490	63	30	17	1934	M	39
e	CRUISING LINER	3,700	415	44	18	12	1904	RC	—
f	CROSS-CHANNEL PASSENGER PACKET	2,600	366	46	13½	22	1927	T	51
g	EXCURSION PADDLE STEAMER	460	232	26	6	20	1894	RC	64
h	TRAIN FERRY	2,900	360	63	12	16	1934	T	55

Propulsion: T Turbines.   M Motor.   RC Steam Reciprocating.

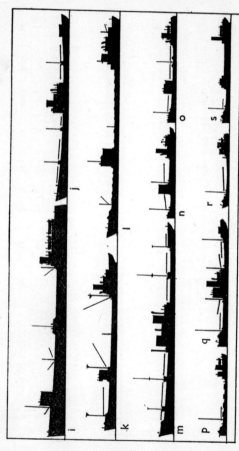

FIG. 9.—Comparative silhouettes of merchant ships—II

COMPARATIVE SILHOUETTES
(Fig. 9)

No.	Type	Gross Register Tonnage	Length overall in feet	Breadth in feet	Draught in feet	Speed in knots	Date of Building	Pro-pulsion	Page
i	WHALE OIL FACTORY SHIP	14,300	550	74	33	11	1930	M	63
j	STANDARD TYPE FREIGHTER	7,176	442	57	28	11	1943	R C	43
k	HEAVY CARGO CARRIER	7,200	440	67	26	11	1926	M	43
l	OIL TANKER	10,000	523	63	28	14	1939	M	57
m	CARGO LINER	6,800	482	61	27	15	1932	M	41
n	COASTER	800	216	27	14	9	1918	R C	49
o	MOTOR LINER COASTER	1,200	265	38	15	12	1935	M	49
p	COASTAL TANKER	800	190	30	12	9	1930	M	58
q	TIMBER CARRIER OR COLLIER	2,000	300	44	18	10	1920	R C	41
r	DUTCH MOTOR COASTER	300	160	25	12	8	1935	M	49
s	FLAT-IRON COLLIER	1,300	250	36	16	11	1932	R C	151

NATIONAL FLAGS AND ENSIGNS (I)

(*See* Plate IV)

UNLESS otherwise stated all these flags are worn on the ensign staff at the stern. Small vessels sometimes wear them at the gaff of the mainmast.

British ensigns are twice as long as they are wide. Some foreign ensigns are similar, but some are much shorter in relation to their width.

In port ensigns are hoisted at 8 a.m. between March and September or at 9 a.m. between September and March, and they are hauled down at sunset. At sea ensigns may be flown as long as there is sufficient light for them to be seen. They must be flown when a ship is entering or leaving port at any time of the day or night. British ships of over fifty tons are compelled by law to carry and wear the national flag.

1. UNION JACK. Worn at the jackstaff of British warships while at anchor. The pilot flag is a Union Jack with a white border, worn at the jackstaff by merchant ships or at the foremast when a pilot is required.

2. WHITE ENSIGN. Ensign of the Royal Navy, worn by H.M. ships, shore establishments, and boats of the Royal Yacht Squadron.

3. RED ENSIGN. National ensign of the British Merchant Navy. Worn by any British-owned ship, yacht, or small boat. Also used as the ensign of Dominions, each distinguished by their emblems, e.g. the stars of Australia. Trinity House, Humber Conservancy, and other institutions also wear this flag with an emblem on the fly. Known as the "Red Duster."

4. BLUE ENSIGN. Worn as the national ensign by merchant ships which have among their crews

28

a certain number of officers and men belonging to the Royal Naval Reserve. Members of certain yacht clubs may by special warrant wear this ensign with the club emblem on the fly. Lloyd's, Custom House, Mersey Docks and Harbour Board, etc., also wear this flag with their badges on the fly.

5. ROYAL AIR FORCE. Worn by R.A.F. Stations, Air Sea Rescue launches, and other vessels belonging to the R.A.F.

6. ADMIRALTY. Worn by fleet auxiliaries and oilers.

7. TRINITY HOUSE. The badge on the fly of the Red Ensign. Used by lighthouse tenders and pilot boats.

8. IRISH LIGHTS. Ensign used in the same way as No. 7 above.

9. COMMISSIONER OF NORTHERN LIGHTS. Lighthouse service of Scotland and the Isle of Man. Worn only when Commissioners are on board lighthouse tenders. Normal ensign is blue with white lighthouse.

10. PAKISTAN. National flag and Merchant Service.

11. INDIA. National flag and Merchant Service ensign. Both this and No. 10 are worn as jacks by the warships of each navy.

12. EIRE. National flag and Merchant Service.

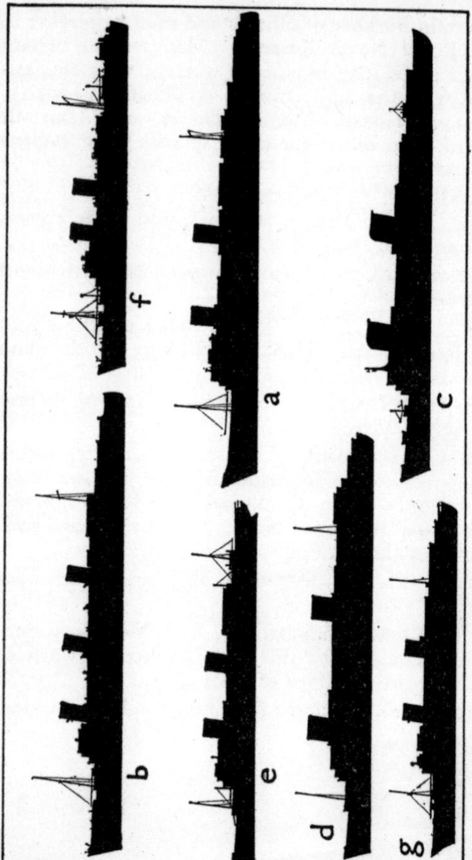

Fig. 10.—Transatlantic passenger liners

TRANSATLANTIC PASSENGER LINER
(Plate XXV)

THE main features of these liners are the immensely long and high superstructure, the comparatively unimportant masts (with perhaps four derricks), the enormous number of lifeboats, and the great length of enclosed promenade deck. The highest promenade deck is sometimes as much as 70 ft. above water level.

In peace-time these ships keep strictly to the routes between their terminal ports—Southampton, Cherbourg, Havre, and New York—simply because their immense size entails special deep-water quays, special passenger, baggage, customs, and other facilities. The "turn-round" may be only a few days, and to ensure the competent and smooth running of these floating luxury hotels, the replenishing of stores, cleaning of accommodation, and many other tasks have to be done at high speed and with great efficiency. In 1956 over a million passengers were carried across the North Atlantic in about seventy liners.

The seven largest liners on the North Atlantic

Name	Flag Date	Gross Tonnage	Overall Length (feet)	Service Speed (knots)	Number of Passengers
a *Queen Elizabeth* .	Br. 1940	83,673	1,031	28·5	2,300
b *Queen Mary* .	Br. 1936	81,237	1,019	28·5	2,040
c *United States* .	U.S.A. 1952	53,329	990	29 35·5 max.	2,000 14,000 troops
d *Liberté, ex-Europa* .	Fr. 1928	51,840	936	23	1,500
e *Ile de France* .	Fr. 1926	44,153	793	23	1,570
f *Mauretania* .	Br. 1939	35,674	772	23	1,170
g *Nieuw Amsterdam* .	Ne. 1938	36,667	758	21·5	1,230
Building 1. *France* . To replace *Liberté*	Fr.	55/60,000	984	30	2,000
2. Sister ship to *United States* . To replace *America*	U.S.A.	53,000	—	—	—
3. *Rotterdam*	Ne.	36,000	—	—	—

31

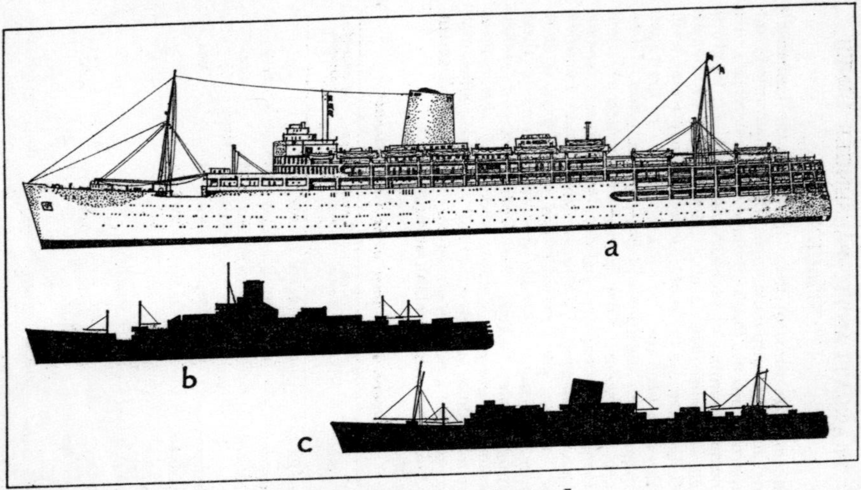

FIG. 11.—Passenger liners—I

PASSENGER LINER
(Plates XX, XXI, XXIV and XXVIII)

As the name suggests, this type of vessel is employed primarily for the carrying of passengers in any part of the world but she is generally designed to carry a small amount of cargo. Size and silhouettes vary considerably and, with recent experiments in funnel design, some companies have adopted a type of funnel which helps identification.

The large drawing shows a passenger liner built for trade between Great Britain, Australia, and New Zealand via the Suez Canal. Her open promenade decks suggest that she is employed in tropical waters; the ships on the North Atlantic routes have more protection against wind and weather.

The outline of the passenger liner may be broken by deck houses, boats, and derricks. The two silhouettes opposite show passenger vessels with quite different shapes although they are approximately the same size. The *Orcades* (b) illustrates the modern tendency to place the tripod mast and funnel rather close together. The *Edinburgh Castle* (c) (and *Pretoria Castle*—Plate XX) carry only half the number of passengers as the *Orcades* but much more cargo—a fact suggested by their larger number of derricks.

Illustrations (FIG. 11)

(a) *Iberia*. Built in 1954 for the P. & O. Line. 29,614 g.t. 718 ft. o.a. Geared turbines, twin screw, speed of 24·9 knots. Accommodation for 1,407 passengers. 4,000 dwt. cargo. Great Britain to Australia and Far East.

(b) *Orcades*. Built in 1948 for the Orient Line. 28,164 g.t. 709 ft. o.a. Geared turbines, twin screw, speed of 21·8 knots. Accommodation for 1,534 passengers on the route from Tilbury to Australia.

(c) *Edinburgh Castle*. Built in 1948 for the Union-Castle Line. 28,705 g.t. 747 ft. o.a. Geared turbines, twin screw, speed of 22 knots. Accommodation for 705 passengers on the Southampton to South Africa Mail service.

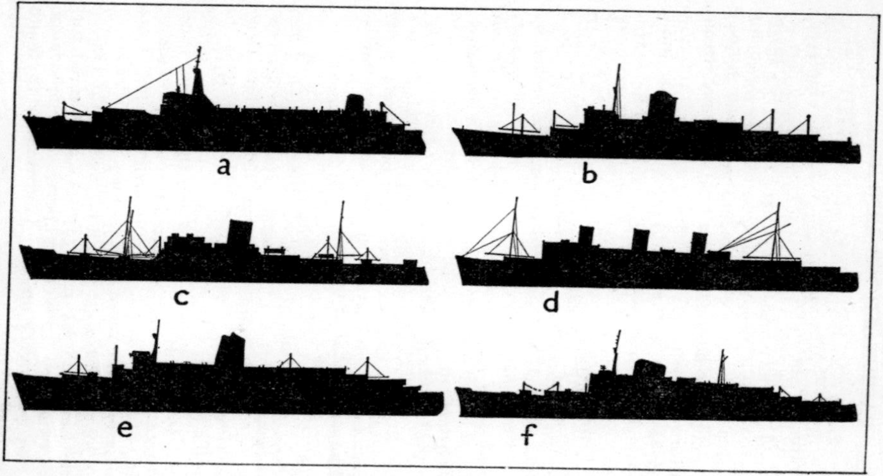

FIG. 12.—Passenger liners—II

The infinite variety of outline is shown in the drawings of six passenger liners. The *Southern Cross* (a) is the first large passenger liner to be built with her engines aft, but the P. & O. Line has already planned a vessel with a similar silhouette. The *Southern Cross* carries no cargo whatsoever and this design, together with the new arrangement of her machinery, allows for much greater scope in planning the large public rooms and unrestricted deck space. The new P. & O. liner will have another new feature; the lifeboats will be inset on the lowest promenade deck instead of on the uppermost deck.

Illustrations (Fig. 12)

	Date	gt.	ft. o.a.	kn.	Passengers
(a) *Southern Cross* Shaw Savill Line	1955	20,203	603	20	1,160
(b) *Saxonia* and three sisters Cunard	1954	21,637	608	20	940
(c) *Rangitane* New Zealand Line	1949	21,867	609	17	403
(d) *Queen of Bermuda* Furness Line	1933	22,501	580	20	731
(e) *Empress of Britain* Canadian Pacific	1956	25,516	640	21	1,050
(f) *Flandre* C.G.T.	1951	20,469	599	23	709
Building *Canberra* P. & O. Largest to Far East	1960	45,000	814	27·5	2,250
Oriana Orient Line		40,000	—	—	—

NATIONAL FLAGS AND ENSIGNS (II)

(See Plate V)

1. France
2. Belgium
3. Netherlands
4. Italy
5. Greece
6. Norway
7. Sweden
8. Finland
9. Denmark
10. Argentine
11. Panama
12. Brazil
13. Portugal
14. U.S.S.R.
15. U.S.A.
16. Spain
17. Japan
18. Iceland

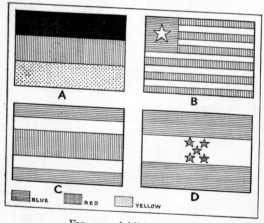

FIG. 13.—Additional flags

A West Germany   C Costa Rica
B Liberia   D Honduras

FLAGS OF CONVENIENCE

Since the last war a large number of merchant ships have been registered under the flags of Panama,

Liberia, Costa Rica and Honduras. These small countries with previously little or no mercantile marine, have shipping laws with much lower standards than those of Great Britain and America. Taxation is considerably less and thus the shipowners are able to operate with better profits when their vessels are registered under flags of convenience. Many big British companies are now operating associated companies under these flags and that of Bermuda. Some of the world's largest tankers are owned by companies flying the Liberian and Panamanian national flags.

FIG. 14.—Modern Silhouettes

1. Norwegian North Sea packet motor ship. 2. American transatlantic steamship. 3. Dutch steam cargo liner. 4 and 5. British passenger steamships. 6. British motor coaster.

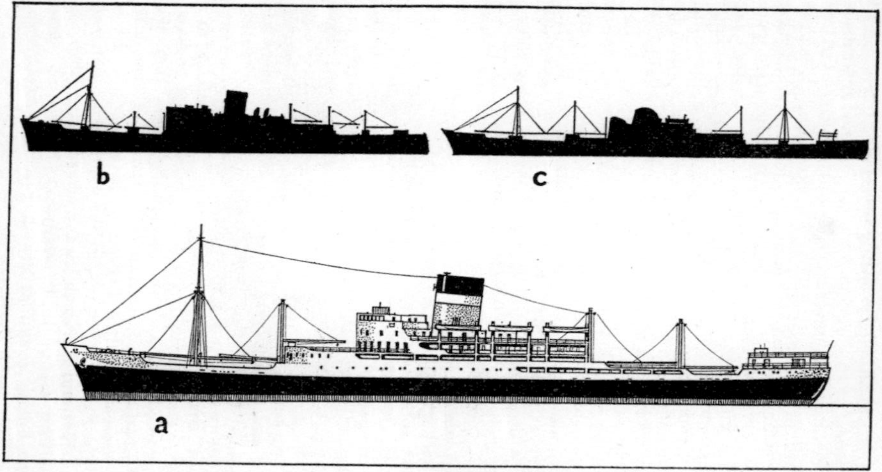

Fig. 15.—Cargo-passenger Liners

CARGO-PASSENGER LINER

(Plate III)

ALTHOUGH most passenger liners do carry some cargo, their main function is to cater for several hundred passengers at a speed between 20 and 30 knots. The smaller intermediate liner is one in which the passengers and the cargo are of equal importance. This type is found on most of the world's trade routes; it is distinguished from the true passenger liner by the much shorter superstructure and greater number of derricks or deck cranes. As a rule the speed is between 15 and 18 knots and the machinery is either steam-turbine or diesel. The new funnel designs have increased the variety of silhouettes, but the tendency is now towards a compact superstructure with a broad and often raked funnel which is sometimes incorporated in the navigation bridge.

The *City of Port Elizabeth* (a) owned by the Ellerman Lines, illustrates this type of liner. Built in 1952 by Vickers-Armstrong on the Tyne, she measures 13,363 tons gross with an overall length of 541 ft. Her Doxford-type diesels and twin screws give her a service speed of just over 16 knots. She has a curved and raked stem and a cruiser stern. She carries 100 passengers between London and South and East Africa.

The Cunard *Parthia* (b) is a vessel of similar length, speed and tonnage but she carries 251 passengers between Liverpool and New York. She is propelled by double-reduction geared turbines and twin screws.

The French *Caledonien* (c) is a similar vessel with a much lower superstructure and a modern type of raked and domed funnel. She is slightly longer than the other two ships but measures a thousand tons less. Her diesels give her a speed of 16 knots and she is employed carrying 241 passengers and cargo between Marseilles and Australia via the Panama canal.

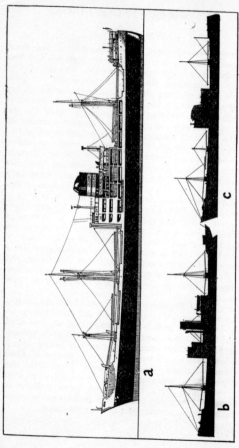

Fig. 16.—Cargo liners

CARGO LINER

(Plate VII)

THE ocean-going general cargo carrier is the most numerous unit of the world's merchant fleets. The cargo liner runs to a fixed time-table between two or more ports on a regular service. Her size may be anything from 3,000 to 10,000 tons gross and her silhouette is capable of many variations in hull form, type of superstructure, position of mast and type of funnel. The speed may be as low as nine and as high as seventeen knots. A *tramp* is not so much a type of ship as a service on which a vessel is employed. The tramp is a general cargo carrier employed to take cargoes from port to port at any time wherever they are offered. She may be away from her home port for a year or more and voyages may be of any length. The tramp's appearance does not differ from the normal cargo liner except that she may have more derricks.

The drawing (Fig. 16a) illustrates a modern cargo liner built for the Clan Line to operate from Birkenhead to South and East Africa. With a length of 502 ft. o.a. and a measurement of 7,698 g.t. her turbines give her a speed of 17 knots and she carries 10,000 tons of cargo and twelve passengers in excellent accommodation. She is a good example of the fast cargo liner. The other two drawings show contrasting types of cargo liners: a 1930 steamship and a 1956 motor ship.

The short-sea trader is a steam or motor ship, usually under 3,000 tons and employed in the North Sea, Baltic or Mediterranean. Engines can be amidships or aft but the latter position is the commonest. The short-sea trader may carry grain or coal in bulk or general cargo and may at times carry a cargo of timber which is piled up on deck as well as fully occupying the holds. Freighters built for this trade have masts and kingposts set against the three islands to allow clear spaces between for the timber deck cargo.

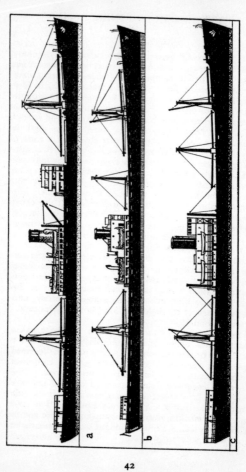

FIG. 17.—Standard types of shelter deck general cargo merchant ships

a

b

c

STANDARD TYPES OF MERCHANT
SHIPS (Plate VII)

During the two world wars thousands of new cargo ships were required to replace those lost by enemy action. Building had to be swift and was much simplified. In the Second World War the designs were better and more pleasing than the ugly American *Hog Island* sheerless type of the First World War. Valuable time was saved by the introduction of prefabrication, the extensive use of welding and standardization of parts.

The American-built *Liberty* type (Fig. 17b) is probably the best known of the second war standard types as there are still hundreds of them still at sea. The 7,000-ton *Liberty* (Plate VII) is flush decked with a short, high superstructure and three masts. The Canadian-built *Fort* and *Park* types (a) and the American-built *Oceans* are similar in size to the *Liberty* but they have split superstructures. The third drawing (c) is of an American-built *Victory* type, 7,500 tons, which is about three knots faster than the above and distinguished by a larger composite superstructure and a long forecastle.

The British standard cargo liner is a 15-knot vessel of almost 10,000 tons gross with a short forecastle, composite superstructure and three masts forward and one aft with kingposts set against the after end of the bridge. Besides heavy cargo-handling machinery and facilities for carrying bulky deck cargoes, she has excellent accommodation for twenty-four passengers.

The United States built a large number of C1 to C4 standard types for their own use. The first three have short, high superstructures and three holds forward and two aft with many variations of masts, kingposts and details of bridge. The C4 has engines aft. The American T2 tanker was a standard type and the British built three standard types of oil tankers which included the *Waves* for the Admiralty. The *Bel* heavy-lift ships with engines aft (page 27) belonged to another class of wartime standard. The Germans produced the successful *Hansa* standard type short-sea trader of 1,900 tons gross.

COLOURS OF SHIPPING COMPANIES

A KEY TO COLOURS OF SHIPPING COMPANIES

The vertical sub-divisions of the hull and ventilator colours indicate alternative schemes within the same company.

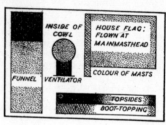

Fig. 18.—*Topsides* refers to the main hull colour and *Boot-topping* to the colour at the water line

ATLANTIC PASSENGER MAIL AND CARGO LINES (Plate VIII)

Fig. No.	Name of Shipping Firm.	Port of Registry, General naming system, Routes.

1. THE CUNARD STEAM-SHIP CO., LTD. Names ending in *ia*, one in *ic*, and two *Queens*. Southampton, Liverpool and London to U.S.A. and Canada. Cargo to Mediterranean and Channel Isles, London to Great Lakes.

2. FURNESS, WITHY AND CO., LTD. London and Liverpool. Misc. names. London, Liverpool and Manchester to New York, Newfoundland, Nova Scotia, and North American Pacific ports.

3. THE UNION-CASTLE MAIL STEAMSHIP CO., LTD. London. Second word: *Castle*. U.K. to South Africa, East Africa and Mauritius via Madeira. London to East Africa. Amalgamated with Clan Line. Black hulls, have white line.

4. ANCHOR LINE, LTD. Glasgow. Names ending in *ia*. Glasgow and Liverpool to New York, India and Pakistan.

5. COMPAGNIE GENERALE TRANSATLANTIQUE, LTD. Havre. Misc. names. Havre and Southampton to New York and West Indies. Mediterranean services.

6. UNITED STATES LINES. New York. First word: *American* except transatlantic liners. New York to Southampton. United Kingdom and Continent to U.S.A. Eastern ports.

7. CANADIAN PACIFIC STEAMSHIPS, LTD. Montreal or London. Some passenger ships: *Empress of.* Some freighters, prefix: *Beaver.* London, Liverpool and Continent to Canada and U.S.A. London to Great Lakes.

8. NORWEGIAN AMERICA LINE. Oslo. Suffix: *fjord.* Oslo, Bergen and Stavanger to Canada, U.S.A. and East Africa.

9. SWEDISH AMERICA LINE. Gothenburg. Suffix: *holm.* Sweden to New York, Halifax and Mexico.

10. ROYAL MAIL LINES, LTD. London. Various names. Some beginning with *A.* Some first word *Highland* (old Nelson Line). London, Liverpool, Southampton, etc., to South America, Central America and North Pacific.

11. ROYAL NETHERLANDS STEAMSHIP Co. (K.N.S.M.). Amsterdam. Mainly Roman names. European ports to Central America.

12. YEOWARD BROS. Liverpool. Spanish words beginning with *A.* Liverpool to Lisbon, Madeira and the Canaries.

13. ITALIA LINE. Genoa. Italian names. Genoa and Naples to America.

14. BLUE STAR LINE, LTD. London. Second word: *Star.* U.K. to S. America, S. Africa and Australasia. Australia and State Settlements—names without *Star.*

15. ELDER DEMPSTER LINES, LTD. Liverpool. African place-names and pioneers of Africa. United Kingdom, Continent, U.S.A. and Canada to West Africa. Some white or grey hulls.

16. FARRELL LINES INC. New York. United States to South Africa. First word: *African.*

17. HOLLAND AMERICA LINE. Rotterdam. Suffix: *dijk* or *dam.* Europe to U.S.A. and West Indies. Some grey hulls.

18. JAMAICA BANANA PRODUCERS' STEAM SHIP Co., LTD. (Kaye, Son and Co. Ltd.). London. First word: *Jamaica* or prefix: *Mar.* Liverpool and Rotterdam to Jamaica and River Plate. *Mar:* black hulls. All now red boot-topping.

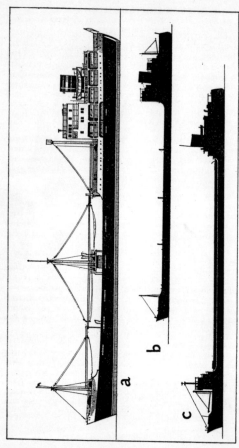

FIG. 19.—Bulk carriers

BULK CARRIERS

THE bulk carrier is a specially designed freighter employed for the exclusive carriage of oil, ore, molasses, latex, cement, sugar, bauxite, phosphates or coal. The oil tanker is described on page 57. The collier is usually a raised quarter deck coaster (Fig. 20) without derricks, as loading and discharging of coal is done by dockside cranes.

The bulk sugar carrier is a type developed in recent years. The *Sugar Importer* (Fig. 19a) is a modern motor ship of 3,960 g.t. carrying about 5,000 tons of sugar from the West Indies to London. She has an overall length of 353 ft. and is driven by two 8-cylinder British Polar diesels. The sugar is discharged by grabs and the hatch covers are of the combined rolling and pivoting type.

The bulk ore carrier is usually a large vessel with engines aft. The drawing (b) shows a British motor ship of 7,000 g.t. and a length of 427 ft. For the reason suggested above in connection with the collier, she has no derricks. The three projections are part of the gear which operates the hinged hatches.

The illustration (c) is the silhouette of a large single-screw turbine ore-carrier, the *Carl Schmedeman* (9,918 g.t.) which carries aluminium ore (bauxite) from Ocho Rios Bay, Jamaica, to Mobile in Alabama. She has stern self-unloading equipment capable of discharging her ore cargo at the rate of 1,400 tons per hour. Like the Great Lakes carriers her bridge is placed on the forecastle (*see* page 151).

Several oil tankers such as the *Sinclair Petrolore* (35,131 g.t.) have been designed to carry return cargoes of ore. Sailing under the Liberian flag (*see* page 36) she has over a million cubic feet of ore space in her bottom and sides with self-unloading gear and two and a half million cubic feet of space for oil. She takes oil from the Persian Gulf to America, sails in ballast to Venezuela to load ore for Japan, and returns to the Gulf for more oil.

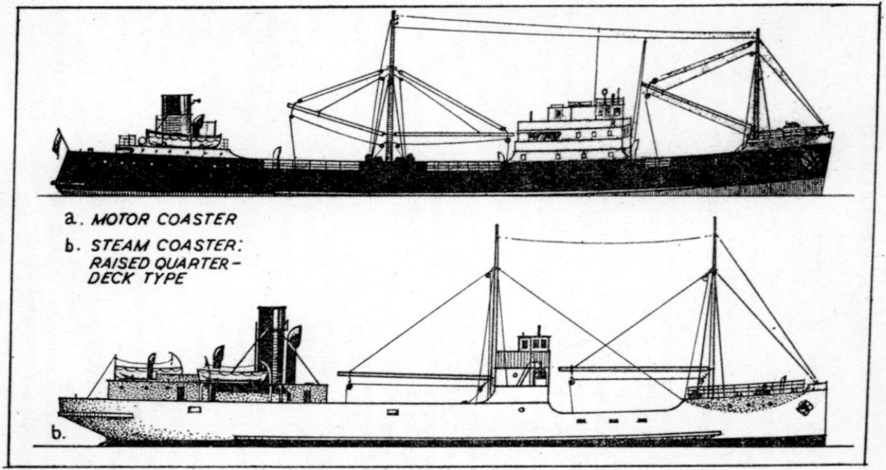

a. MOTOR COASTER

b. STEAM COASTER:
   RAISED QUARTER–
   DECK TYPE

Fig. 20 (a).—Coasters

THE COASTER

(*See* Plates VI and XIV)

THE coaster can be seen anywhere around our coasts, in any port, large or small, or tied up at a lonely up-river quay. Generally she is an all-purpose cargo carrier, although some coasters run to a regular time-table between certain ports and might be classed as specialized "liners." Many coasters are employed as colliers either on regular coastal or irregular short-sea routes. At the other extreme is the tiny *puffer*, ubiquitous on the West Coast of Scotland, where she is the only means of transporting cargo between many of the islands.

The average coaster is about 200 ft. in length with a gross tonnage of something under 2,000, and has powerful derricks and deck machinery capable of handling a variety of cargoes in small ports where there is little or no quayside machinery. Usually the machinery is aft so that the shaft tunnel is short and does not take up valuable space. Some vessels have a raised quarter deck—that is, the deck from the bridge to the poop is several feet higher than the forward well deck (*See* Fig. 20a). This gives a better trim when the ship is fully loaded. All coasters have a rubbing strake on each side of the hull to protect it from damage by bumping while tied up to a quay wall. Some modern motor coasters have good cabin accommodation for twelve passengers.

FIG. 20 (b).—Dutch Coaster

During recent years the Dutch motor coaster has become a common type in European waters. Developed in Holland from the *schuyt* for operating in very shallow estuaries, rivers, and canals, she has a shallow draft, engines and accommodation aft, a large hold, electric cargo machinery, and a strong hull to enable her to lie well on the ground at low water. It is quite usual for the skipper of a Dutch-owned coaster to live on board with his family in spotlessly clean accommodation.

49

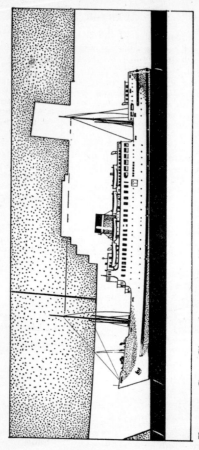

FIG. 21.—Cross-Channel passenger ship operating on a short sea route at a speed of over 20 knots. Turbine driven, she has a length of 366 ft. and a tonnage of 2,600 gross. As a day steamer, she carries 2,600 passengers. For comparison of size she is shown here alongside a transatlantic liner.

CROSS-CHANNEL PACKET
(See Plate XXIX)

THE cross-Channel steamer or motor ship is similar in appearance and in function to the much larger passenger liners. She carries a large number of passengers and mail and a small amount of cargo on routes which demand accurate timing to fit in with train services. The ships built for day crossings carry about 1,500 passengers and have eight or ten lifeboats. The night ships, usually on a longer route, have accommodation for about 500 passengers. The *Duke of Lancaster* (*see* Plate XXIX) recently built for the British Transport Commission's Heysham–Belfast route, is a good example of a cross-Channel packet. She has accommodation for 1,800 passengers, mail, baggage, newspapers, motor cars, and general cargo.

The cross-Channel packets have high-powered engines to maintain a speed of about 20 knots in all weathers. The prevailing weather conditions of the route have an important effect on the design of the ship. Many of the routes, especially across the English Channel, are noted for bad weather although the distances are quite short. The introduction of Denny-Brown stabilizers on the latest cross-Channel ships has reduced rolling.

The following are some cross-Channel routes:

DAY	Dover – Calais : Ostend – Dover : Liverpool–Isle of Man : Stranraer–Larne
NIGHT	Harwich–Hook : Liverpool–Belfast : Glasgow–Belfast
DAY OR NIGHT	Weymouth–Channel Islands : Seattle–Vancouver – Victoria : Buenos Aires–Montevideo
DAY AND NIGHT PASSAGE	Harwich–Esbjerg : Newcastle–Bergen

Most of the crossings from the British Isles to Ireland and the Continent take less than 24 hours.

COLOURS OF SHIPPING COMPANIES

PASSENGER, MAIL, AND CARGO LINES TO PACIFIC AND FAR EAST

(*See* Plate IX)

1. BIBBY BROS. & CO. Liverpool. English shires. Liverpool to Mediterranean, Ceylon and Burma. Trooping.

2. SHAW SAVILL AND ALBION CO., LTD. London. Maori names. Suffix: *ic* and various. London to South Africa, Australia and New Zealand. *Southern Cross* has grey hull and pale green upper marks.

3. FEDERAL STEAM NAVIGATION CO., LTD. London. English counties. United Kingdom to America, Australia and New Zealand.

4. THE NEW ZEALAND SHIPPING CO., LTD. London. Maori names. London and Southampton to New Zealand via Panama.

5. BRITISH INDIA STEAM NAVIGATION CO., LTD. London. Indian names ending in *a*. London, Middlesbrough to East Africa, Australia, and local Indian services. Passenger liners with white hulls and black line.

6. ORIENT STEAM NAVIGATION CO., LTD. London. Names beginning with *O*. Tilbury to Mediterranean, Ceylon and Australia. Black "admiralty" top to funnel.

7. PENINSULAR AND ORIENTAL STEAM NAVIGATION CO. London. Oriental names. Tilbury to Mediterranean, India, Ceylon, Australia, China and Japan. (Some black funnels.)

8. THE PACIFIC STEAM NAVIGATION CO. Liverpool. South American names. Liverpool to Central America, Panama and west South America.

9. THE ABERDEEN AND COMMONWEALTH LINE, LTD. London. *Bays* in Australia. London via Mediterranean to Ceylon and Australia.

10. ROYAL INTER OCEAN LINES. Amsterdam. Some beginning with *Tji*. Far East, South Africa and South America.

11. MESSAGERIES MARITIMES. Marseilles. French celebrities. Marseilles to Egypt, East Africa, Ceylon and the Far East.

12. UNION STEAM SHIP CO. OF NEW ZEALAND, LTD. Wellington or London. Maori names beginning with *K* or *W*, and suffix: *ic*. London, Southampton to New Zealand. Pacific Services.

13. ELLERMAN LINES, LTD. (City Line). London. *City of*. United Kingdom to India.

14. ALFRED HOLT & Co. (Blue Funnel Line). Liverpool. Names of Greek heroes. Liverpool, Glasgow, Swansea to Indonesia and Far East.

15. LLOYD TRIESTINO. Trieste. Italian personal names. Trieste to Far East, India, Africa and Australia. Funnel has blue top and narrow blue band.

16. GRACE LINE INC. New York. First word: *Santa*. New York to Central America. San Francisco to Pacific ports. Also grey hulls.

17. AMERICAN PRESIDENT LINES LTD. San Francisco. First word: *President*. New York to Central America, San Francisco to Pacific, China, Japan and East Indies. Also grey hulls.

18. P. HENDERSON & Co. Glasgow. Burmese names. Glasgow and Liverpool to India and Ceylon via Mediterranean.

Arrangement by Funnel Colours

Colours of funnel	Plate VIII	Plate IX	Plate XII	Plate XIII	Plate XVI	Plate XVII
Black	4	7, 11, 18		7	1, 2	8
Black with white or coloured bands	2, 11	5	5, 6, 11	1, 5, 8, 15, 18		6, 12, 14, 15, 16, 17
Black with white or coloured bands and/or markings	12	10	8, 16, 18	3, 10, 13		1, 3, 4, 5, 7, 11, 13, 18
Buff or yellow . .	10, 15	4, 6, 7, 8, 9	3	6, 9	3, 4, 7	10
Buff or yellow with coloured bands or markings	7, 8, 9, 16, 17			2, 4, 17	5	1, 3
Buff or yellow with black top		2	2, 13		6, 7, 8	
Buff or yellow with black top, coloured bands and/or markings		13	1, 9	11, 12, 14		
Yellow with blue top		15				
Red with black top . .	3, 5		10		9, 10, 11, 12	
Red with black top and coloured bands	1	12	15		13, 15	9
Red with black top, coloured bands and markings	14	3	4, 12		14	
Red with coloured top .	6				16	
White						2
White with black top .						
White with black top and coloured bands	13					
Blue with various bands .	18	14, 17	14	16	17, 18	
Green with various bands and/or markings		16	7, 17			
Pink with black top .		1				

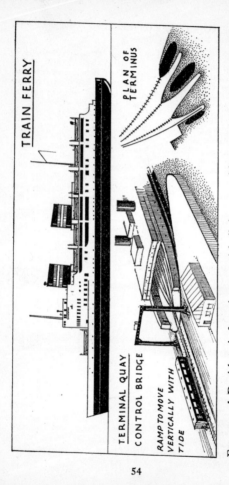

TRAIN FERRY

PLAN OF TERMINUS

TERMINAL QUAY
CONTROL BRIDGE

RAMP TO MOVE
VERTICALLY WITH
TIDE

FIG. 22.—A Danish train ferry (2,950 g.t.) built in 1951 with a speed of 16½ knots for the service between Nyborg and Korsor. The lower drawings show the pivoted ramp necessary in tidal waters.

TRAIN FERRY
(Plate XI)

THE train ferry is used only on a few short sea routes. With her broad beam, high superstructure, and lack of sheer and derricks she is unmistakable. The essential feature is the long, clear deck equipped with two or more rail tracks, and with access at one or both ends of the vessel. The boiler flues are sometimes taken up to twin funnels placed near the ship's sides, so that the rail deck may be as large as possible.

To enable the deck rails to line up correctly with those on shore the hull is shaped to fit exactly into a terminal dock with a pivoted ramp which rises and falls with the tide.

The train ferry has passenger accommodation and dining saloons. On some overnight services the passengers remain in the train sleeping cars.

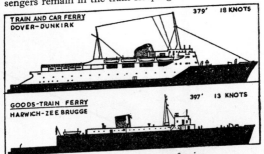

FIG. 23.—Miscellaneous ferries

Train ferries carry London–Paris trains from England to the Continent via Dover and Dunkirk. In Denmark, with its numerous islands, the train ferry is an important part of the railway system. In the North American Lakes there are many train ferries, and in order to maintain a full twelve-months' service these are fitted as icebreakers. Large train ferries carry 100 loaded wagons between New Orleans and Cuba, New Orleans–New Jersey, Texas City–New York.

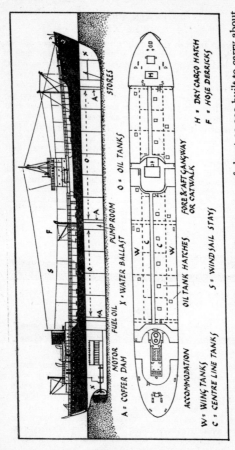

A = COFFER DAM

MOTOR   FUEL OIL   PUMP ROOM   STORES

X = WATER BALLAST   O = OIL TANKS

OIL TANK HATCHES

FORE & AFT GANGWAY
OR CATWALK

S = WINDSAIL STAYS

H = DRY CARGO HATCH

F = HOSE DERRICKS

ACCOMMODATION

W = WING TANKS
C = CENTRE LINE TANKS

Fig. 24.—An ocean-going tanker with a dwt. tonnage of about 30,000 built to carry about 28,500 tons of oil. She has a length of 523 ft. and a service speed of about 15 knots.

TANKER

(*See* Plate X)

The specialized carrier of oil in bulk is now one of the most important vessels in the world's merchant fleets. She is distinguished from the general cargo carrier by her long, low hull, island bridge, and the after position of her engines. The three islands—forecastle, bridge, and poop—are connected by light fore-and-aft bridges called *catwalks*. These are necessary as the low deck is frequently awash. As the tank tops are all watertight there is no danger of flooding when this happens. Most tankers are motor driven, especially the recently built ones. The steam tanker is easily recognized by the tall funnel right at the forward end of the poop.

Two longitudinal bulkheads and many transverse bulkheads divide the hull into numerous tanks. Each tank has a watertight hatch and a ventilator, and is connected by pipeline to the pumping rooms. In two or more positions are double bulkheads, providing narrow air space, called coffer dams. These coffer dams give strength and lessen the danger of fire spreading from the forecastle or engine rooms to the tanks. The dangerous swilling effect of a liquid cargo is minimized by the smallness of the tanks.

Tankers which carry lubricating or crude oil are fitted with internal heating systems to keep the cargo at the right temperature, otherwise it might have to be dug out instead of being pumped out. The danger of fire is less with this type of oil, but petrol and other highly inflammable spirits require careful handling.

During the 1950s new tankers have grown larger and larger so that the vessel of 30,000 tons dwt. has become almost commonplace and the latest ships have surpassed 750 ft. in length and a gross tonnage of 30,000. The tanker *Spyros Niarchos* and her sister ship (Plate X) belong to this category. Even larger tankers are building and it is expected that the newest ships will be able to carry 100,000 tons of oil. It is more economical to carry cargoes in these monster tankers but facilities at terminal ports will limit their routes; they will be unable to pass through the Suez Canal with a full load. Tankers of 500,000 tons dwt. are now discussed.

COASTAL TANKER
(*See* Plate X)

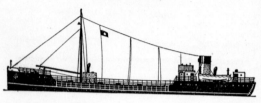

FIG. 25.—A coastal tanker

THE coastal tanker is a smaller version of the ocean-going tanker. Her trips are usually short and she may be employed for many months or years on the same route between ports only a few sailing hours apart. The ocean-going tanker discharges her cargo at large oil installations, and fleets of coastal tankers distribute the oil, petrol, or spirits to smaller depots.

The coastal tanker generally has her navigating bridge on the poop, leaving a clear space between the poop and the forecastle. The tank top in this space is at two levels; the centre section is a few feet higher, forming what is known as a trunk deck. The lower level on each side is only a few inches above the water-line when the vessel is carrying a full cargo. The single mast may carry one light derrick for loading stores or the hoses.

Some coastal tankers are driven by steam engines, others by motors. The drawing (above) is of a vessel of about 800 tons with a length of 180 ft. overall, driven by diesel engines.

FRUIT CARRIER

FIG. 26.—Fruit carrier: 354 ft. o.a., 3,600 g.t., 15 knots

ALTHOUGH the fruit carrier's special equipment is internal she is distinctive in appearance. Equipped to carry fruit at certain low temperatures she is usually a small fast motor ship with a short compact superstructure. She is painted white and often has a long forecastle extending right up to the bridge. She is employed on routes between the West Indies and Europe, California and Europe, and the Caribbean and New York. On the latter route fruit carriers have excellent accommodation for about 200 passengers.

The British and Norwegians were the first to develop this type of vessel and, at the outbreak of the last war, the Germans fitted some of their fruit carriers as commerce raiders. Their handy size and high speed made them admirable for this purpose.

The MEAT CARRIER is another important freighter with special refrigerating machinery for carrying frozen and chilled meat between Australia and New Zealand and Europe. She has no special external characteristics as she is also a general cargo carrier.

COLOURS OF SHIPPING COMPANIES

BRITISH PASSENGER AND CARGO LINES
(*See* Plate XII)

1. THE SHELL PETROLEUM CO., LTD. London. Names of shells.

2. ANDREW WEIR, LONDON, LTD. (Bank Line). London. Suffix: *bank*. Many freighter services all over the world.

4. BRITISH TANKER CO., LTD. London. First word *British*. United Kingdom and Continent from Persian Gulf.

5. THOS. & JNO. BROCKLEBANK, LTD. Liverpool. Indian names beginning with *M*. United Kingdom and Continent to Ceylon and India.

6. CLAN LINE STEAMERS, LTD. London. First word: *Clan*. United Kingdom to South and East Africa, Ceylon, India and Pakistan. World wide services. Amalgamated with Union-Castle.

7. PALM LINE, LIMITED. London. U.K./ Continent to and from West Africa. (Range of ports, Dakar–Angola.)

8. EAGLE OIL AND SHIPPING CO., LTD. London. First word: *San*. Mexican Gulf and United Kingdom.

9. ELLERMAN LINES (Hall Line). Liverpool. *City of*. United Kingdom to South and East Africa and India.

10. GLEN LINE, LTD. (Glen and Shire Line.) London. Prefix: *Glen* or suffix: *shire*. United Kingdom to Continent and Far East.

11. T. & J. HARRISON, LTD. Liverpool. Professions and occupations. United Kingdom to South and East Africa, India, West Indies and Central America.

12. ATHEL LINE, LTD. (United Molasses Co., Ltd.). London. Prefix: *Athel*. World wide tanker services.

13. H. HOGARTH & SONS. Glasgow. First word: *Baron*. Glasgow to Lisbon and Huelva. General trading.

14. LAMPORT AND HOLT LINE, LTD. Liverpool. Famous artists, writers, etc. United Kingdom and New York to Brazil and River Plate.

15. PORT LINE, LTD. London. Prefix: *Port*. United Kingdom to Australia via the Cape and New Zealand via the Panama Canal.

16. PRINCE LINE, LTD. (Furness, Withy). London. Second word: *Prince*. U.S.A. to Brazil and River Plate, Far East and round the world. United Kingdom to the Mediterranean.

17. ROPNER LINE (Ropner Shipping Co., Ltd. and Sir R. Ropner & Co., Ltd.). West Hartlepool. Suffix: *by* or *pool*. U.K. to Florida and U.S.A., Gulf ports and general tramping.

18. RUNCIMAN (London) LTD. (Moor Lines). Newcastle-on-Tyne. Suffix: *moor*. Tramping.

FIG. 27.—*Burgee of the British and Commonwealth Shipping Group.* The Union-Castle Line (Plate VIII-3), Clan Line (Plate XII-6), Bullard King & Co., Ltd., and other subsidiary companies are amalgamated under the title of British and Commonwealth Shipping Company. Ships of the various companies fly this burgee above their own individual house flags.

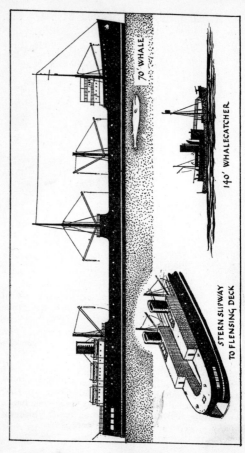

70' WHALE

140' WHALECATCHER

STERN SLIPWAY
TO FLENSING DECK

Fig. 28.—Whale oil factory ship

WHALE OIL FACTORY SHIP

THIS is a form of large tanker, serving in the first place as a depot ship for a fleet of whale-catchers (Fig. 70c) and, in the second, as a cargo ship carrying the products of the whale fisheries to home ports. She may be specially designed for her purpose like the one illustrated in Fig. 28, or she may be a converted freighter or passenger liner. Since the war a number of new vessels have been built in Great Britain. Some of the recent ships are equipped with an amphibian aircraft for spotting the whales.

The factory ship is a large vessel with high freeboard, engines aft, a navigating bridge often right forward, a slipway in the stern, and twin funnels. The one illustrated has a gross tonnage of 14,300 tons and a length of 500 ft. She maintains a speed of about 11 knots. As she has diesel engines she is capable of remaining at sea for many months without refuelling.

The large ships spend the whole of the Antarctic summer in the whaling grounds, leaving Europe about October and returning in the spring.

The whales are harpooned from the small catchers, and the carcases are towed to the mother ship and hauled up through the slipway in the stern on to the large clear flensing deck. The ship is fitted with powerful hauling gear so that the whales are easily moved about the deck. They are cut up and disposed of to various parts of the ship, to be stored as oil or as one of the by-products.

At present the largest factory ship is the *Willem Barendsz (II)*. Dutch owned, she has a gross tonnage of 26,830, a length of 677 ft., a speed of 14 knots and carries a helicopter.

PADDLE STEAMER
(Plates VI and XXXII)

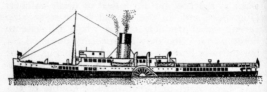

FIG. 29.—An excursion paddle steamer built in 1937, length 200 ft., 600 g.t. operating in the summer in the Bournemouth area

THE paddle steamer is familiar to the thousands of holidaymakers who visit resorts in the Clyde (Plates VI and XXXII), Bristol Channel, and on the South Coast.

She is the only survivor of sea-going paddle steamers; river steamers (page 67) and a few old tugs are still paddle-driven. The paddles allow the steamer to make quick turns and rapid manœuvres alongside piers.

The paddle steamer usually has one slender mast with no derricks, and has a long superstructure with many public rooms and clear deck spaces to accommodate as many as two thousand day passengers.

About thirty of these vessels are still used in the summer months around the British coasts, and of this number about a dozen are approximately fifty years old. In spite of their age several of these paddle steamers maintain a speed of 20 knots.

POWER YACHTS

As a rule the term "yacht" is applied to almost any type of pleasure vessel whether she is propelled by sail, steam, or diesel. The large luxury yacht is expensive to buy and to maintain. Numerous in the early part of the century the graceful steam yachts (a) have been replaced by the low sleek motor yacht (d) smaller in size and more economical to run. Since the war many ex-*Fairmile* naval launches (b) have been converted for private use and many are also employed on public services such as the summer runs between Poole, Bournemouth, and Swanage.

The Pilot Cutter is a yacht-like vessel which may be mistaken for a pleasure craft although she usually has large letters or numerals painted on her topsides. She has accommodation for a number of pilots and her duty is to lie off the entrance to a large port—such as the Thames or Mersey—to supply pilots for the incoming ships and take on board those who are leaving their outgoing ships. One of the latest British pilot boats is the *Edmund Gardner* built for the Mersey Docks and Harbour Board. She is a diesel-electric vessel with a length of 165 ft. o.a., a speed of just over 13 knots and accommodation for 32 pilots. The drawing (c) shows a Belgian vessel of the same type.

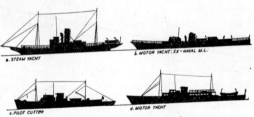

a. STEAM YACHT

b. MOTOR YACHT: EX-NAVAL M.L.

c. PILOT CUTTER

d. MOTOR YACHT

FIG. 30.—Power yachts

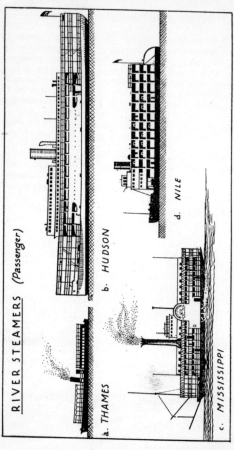

RIVER STEAMERS (Passenger)

a. THAMES

b. HUDSON

c. MISSISSIPPI

d. NILE

FIG. 31.—Various types of river steamers

RIVER PASSENGER STEAMERS

THE river passenger steamer is unlike other types of ship. She carries a large number of passengers for comparatively short distances in shallow water; sometimes with overnight accommodation. The superstructure is unusually long and high. The steamers generally have a very shallow draft, but as they work in sheltered waters their excessive top-hamper and lack of seaworthy qualities do not matter.

Passenger steamers of this type can be seen on most large rivers and estuaries where the water is an important arterial highway. Besides the four rivers mentioned below, the Niger, Volga, St. Lawrence, Yangtze, and Rhine also have interesting craft. Perhaps the best-known estuary steamers in the country are the Mersey ferries, owned by the Wallasey and Birkenhead Corporation.

Illustrations (Fig. 31)

(a) THAMES. The small Thames steamer, 105 ft. long, can carry 400 passengers. Her hinged funnel is lowered at each low bridge in the same manner as that of the flat-iron collier seen on the tidal waters of the same river.

(b) HUDSON. On this American river there are many large fast passenger steamers of this type. The newest ships have more closed-in superstructure and are more streamlined.

(c) MISSISSIPPI. This vanishing craft is associated with the more romantic aspects of North American history. It has tall twin funnels (smokestacks) with serrated tops, and either side or stern paddles in boxes, profusely decorated like many other parts of the ship, with typical "Victorian" decoration.

(d) NILE. The Egyptian river steamer is either a stern-wheeler or a side-paddler with three or four decks which stretch the full length of the hull. Numerous awnings give protection from the sun's heat. The drawing is of an Assuan stern-wheeler, about 150 ft. in length, fitted with cabins and public rooms for day and night travel.

COLOURS OF SHIPPING COMPANIES

FOREIGN PASSENGER AND CARGO LINES
(*See* Plate XIII)

1. WILH. WILHEMSEN. Oslo. Names beginning with *T*. Norway to U.S.A., South Africa and Far East. New York to Far East.

2. FRED OLSEN & Co. Oslo. Names beginning with *B*. Norway to United Kingdom and Continent, Canaries, U.S.A. and Mediterranean.

3. JOHNSON LINE. Stockholm. Surname *Johnson* and South American place-names. Sweden and Poland to South America and North Pacific.

4. SWEDISH EAST ASIATIC Co., LTD. Gothenburg. Oriental names. Scandinavia to India, Pakistan, Philippines and Japan.

5. UNITED STEAMSHIP Co. (Forenede Dampskibs-Selskab, Det.). Copenhagen. Personal and place-names. Scandinavia to U.S.A. and South America, Continental services.

6. EAST ASIATIC Co., LTD. Copenhagen. Eastern place-names. Scandinavia to Far East, India, South Africa and North Pacific. Several motor-ships without funnels (page 151).

7. ROYAL ROTTERDAM LLOYD (Wm. Ruys and Zonen). Rotterdam. Netherlands East Indies place-names. Europe to Far East.

8. UNITED NETHERLANDS NAVIGATION Co. (V.N.S.). Hague. Suffix: *kerk* or *fontein*. Continental ports to South East Africa and Far East.

9. LLOYD ROYAL (Maritime Belge). Antwerp. Passenger ships. Suffix: *ville*. Freighters: African names or suffix: *ier*. Belgium to U.S.A., South America, West Africa and India.

10. AMERICAN EXPORT LINES INC. New York. Prefix: *Ex.* U.S.A. to Mediterranean, Black Sea, North Africa and India.

11. UNITED FRUIT CO. Boston. **Central** American names. New York, New Orleans to Central America and West Indies.

12. HAMBURG-AMERICA LINE. Hamburg.

13. NIARCHOS GROUP. Several companies operating oil tankers under the flags of Greece, Liberia, and Honduras. Own some of world's largest tankers.

14. MOORE-McCORMACK LINES INC. New York. Misc. names. U.S.A. and Canada to Scandinavia, West Indies and Central America.

15. BERGEN STEAMSHIP CO., LTD. Bergen. Classical Roman names. Norway to most European ports, Canada, Baltic and West Africa. One of the earliest companies to operate pleasure cruises.

16. RIO DE LA PLATA, S.A. (Dodero Line). Buenos Aires. Misc. names. Passenger and cargo between the Plate and Europe. Large passenger liners have D on flag instead of RP.

17. POLISH OCEAN LINES, Gdynia. Misc. names. Gydnia to North and South America and Near East.

18. JAPAN MAIL STEAMSHIP CO., LTD. (Nippon Yusen K.). Tokyo. Names of Japanese merchant ships always have second word *Maru.* Japan, India, Pakistan, North America, Europe.

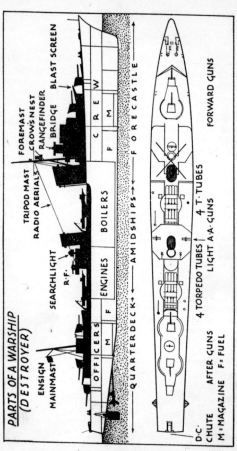

PARTS OF A WARSHIP
(DESTROYER)

FOREMAST
CROW'S NEST
RANGEFINDER
BRIDGE
BLAST SCREEN

TRIPOD MAST
RADIO AERIALS

SEARCHLIGHT

R.F.

ENSIGN
MAINMAST

OFFICERS
M   F
ENGINES

BOILERS

C R E W
F   M

←QUARTERDECK→←AMIDSHIPS→←FORECASTLE→

FORWARD GUNS

4 T. TUBES
LIGHT A.A. GUNS

4 TORPEDO TUBES

D.C.
CHUTE   AFTER GUNS   F = FUEL
M = MAGAZINE

Fig. 32.—Parts of a World War II destroyer

70

WARSHIPS

GENERAL CHARACTERISTICS

COLOUR. It is usual for all navies to paint their warships and auxiliaries grey. The particular grey depends on the part of the world in which the ships operate. In wartime the ships are "dazzle" painted in patches of greys, browns, and blues to break up the outline by camouflage. These patterns and colours vary with the operational area.

GENERAL APPEARANCE. In wartime merchant ships also are painted grey, but the warship is easily distinguished from the freighter by her long, low hull broken by isolated gun houses and control towers, and by the piling up of superstructure around the foremast and bridge. The deck line may be flush or at two levels, but, unlike the freighter, the warship never has a raised deck at the stern.

PROPORTION. The ratio between length and beam varies in each type of warship. The battleship had a length seven times, the carrier eight times, the cruiser nine to ten times, and the destroyer about ten times the beam. The average merchant ship's length is about eight times the beam. The latter ship has parallel sides for the greater part of her length, but the warship has an elliptical or a tapering shape like the destroyer illustrated in Fig. 32.

PROPULSION. Warships are usually propelled by steam turbines and oil-fired water-tube boilers. They are much cleaner, quieter, and more efficient than the reciprocating engines. Outstanding exceptions were the diesel-engined armoured ships (pocket battleships) of the Germans. Diesel engines gave these lone raiders a remarkably wide operational range of 10,000 miles. Diesels are used for a new type of frigate and gas turbines, as yet fitted only to patrol boats, are still in their infancy. Nuclear power, already used for submarines, is envisaged for other types of warships.

SUBDIVISION OF HULL. The merchant ship must, by law, have her hull subdivided by a number of watertight transverse bulkheads but the warship has a much

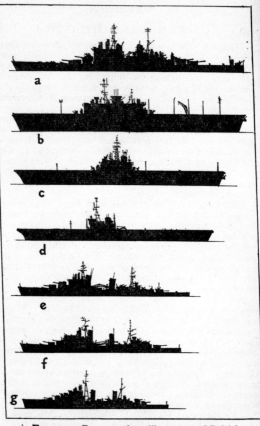

a

b

c

d

e

f

g

FIG. 33.—Comparative silhouettes of British
warships—(I)

greater subdivision by longitudinal and transverse bulkheads. Essential openings in these bulkheads are closed by watertight doors during action. All ships are designed to remain afloat after a certain number of their watertight compartments have been flooded through accident or naval action. The destroyers and small warships are too small to be subdivided by longitudinal bulkheads.

PROTECTION. The battleship was protected amidships by armour plating up to sixteen inches in thickness, but the average cruiser has only three to four inches of armour with about two inches thickness of deck plating. The aircraft carrier is a little more heavily armoured, but the fleet escorts, destroyers, and smaller warships have no armour at all.

COMPARATIVE SILHOUETTES OF BRITISH WARSHIPS

(Fig. 33)

No.	Ship	Standard tonnage	Length o.a.	Sea Speed	Armament	Page ref.
a	Battleship *Vanguard*	44,500	814	28	8—15-in., 16—5·25-in., 64—40-mm.	81
b	Fleet Aircraft Carrier, *Eagle*	36,800	804	31	16—4·5-in., 58—40-mm., 80–110 aircraft	79
c	Aircraft Carrier *Albion*	22,000	738	28	26—40-mm., 45 aircraft	79
d	Light Aircraft Carrier, *Glory* class	13,190	695	24	29—40-mm., 35 aircraft	79
e	Cruiser *Southampton* class	9,100	591	32	9—6-in., 8—4-in. A.A., 6—21-in. tubes up to 18—40-mm.	86
f	Cruiser *Superb*	9,000	555	29	9—6-in., 10—4-in., 6—21-in. tubes 40-mm. and pom-poms	87
g	Cruiser *Dido* class	5,770	512	32	8/10—5·25-in. up to 12—40-mm., 6—21-in. tubes	87

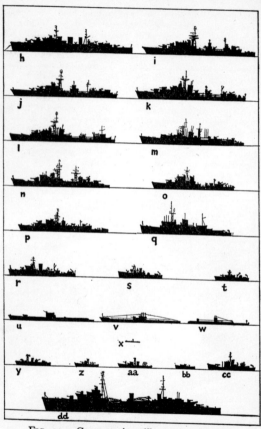

FIG. 34.—Comparative silhouettes of British
warships—(II)

74

COMPARATIVE SILHOUETTES OF BRITISH WARSHIPS

(Fig. 34)

No.	Ship	Standard tonnage	Length o.a.	Speed	Armament	Page ref.
h	Fast minelayer *Manxman* class	2,650	418	40	4/6—4-in., 6—40-mm. 108 mines	107
i	Fleet Escort Ship *Daring* class	2,610	390	30	6—4.5-in., 6—40-mm. 10—21-in. tubes, A/S squid, triple-barrelled D/C mortar	89
j	Fleet Anti-Submarine Escort *Weapon* class	2,000	365	30·75	4—4-in., 6—40-mm., 10—21-in. tubes, 2—A/S squids	89
k	Destroyer *Battle* class	2,460	379	31·54	5—4.5-in., 8—40-mm., 10—21-in. tubes, A/S squid	91
l	Fast Anti-submarine frigate "T" class	1,730	362	31·25	2—4-in., 7—40-mm., 4—21-in. tubes, 2—A/S squids	93
m	Fast Anti-submarine frigate "R" class	2,000	358	31·25	2—4-in., 6—40-mm., 4—21-in. tubes, 2 limbers (i.e. rapid squids)	93
n	Anti-Aircraft Frigate *Leopard* class (diesel)	1,738	340	21	4—4.5-in., 2—40-mm., 1—A/S squid	93
o	Frigate *Hunt* class	1,037	280	25	4—4-in., 4—2-pr.pm., 2—20- or 40-mm., 2—21-in. tubes	93
p	Frigate *Bay* class	1,580	307	19	4—4-in., 40-mm., 1—A/S squid, 4—D.C.T.	93
q	Survey Ship 1954 *Vidal* (Diesel)	1,940	315	?	4—3-pdr. D.C.T. (1 helicopter)	107
r	Ocean Mine-sweeper, *Algerine* class	c. 1,040	235	16	1—4-in., 1/4—40-mm., or up to 8—20-mm., 4—D.C.T. or squid	97
s	Coastal Mine-sweeper *Ton* class	360	152	15	1—40-mm., 2—20-mm.	97
t	Inshore Mine-sweepers, *Ham* class (wooden hulls)	c. 100	106	?	1—40-mm., 1—20-mm.	97
u	Submarine *Porpoise* class	c. 1,500	295			95

No.	Ship	Standard tonnage	Length o.a.	Sea Speed	Armament	Page ref.
v	Submarine A class	1,120/1,385	281	19/8	8—21-in. tubes, 7—M.G.s	95
w	Submarine S class	814/1,000	217	14½/9–12	6—21-in. tubes	95
x	Submarine Midget type	30	54	6	?	95
y	Fast Patrol Boat Bold class	130	123	40	2—4·5-in., 1—40-mm., or 4—21-in. tubes	99
z	Fast Patrol Boat Gay class	50	75	30/35	1—4·5-in., 1—40-mm., or 2—21-in. tubes	99
aa	Seaward Defence Boat Ford class	110	117	18	1—40-mm., A/S squid or D.C.T.	99
bb	Seaward Defence Boat HDML type	46	72	11	1—3-pdr. or 1—40-mm., 1—20-mm.	99
cc	Anti-Submarine and Minesweeping trawler Isles class	550	164	12	Various light A.A.	99
dd	Depot Ship (Destroyer)	11,000	621	17	8—4·5 in.	101

COLOURS OF SHIPPING COMPANIES

BRITISH COASTAL AND CONTINENTAL CARGO AND PASSENGER SERVICES—(I)

(Plate XVI)

1. CLYDE SHIPPING CO., LTD. Glasgow. Names of lighthouses. Coastal services. Tugs.

2. GEO. GIBSON & CO., LTD. Leith. Place names of the Scottish Border country. Coastal and short sea services Leith, Grangemouth, Dundee–Rotterdam, etc. Crossed flags on black funnel for Abbotsford only.

3. THE NORTH OF SCOTLAND, ORKNEY AND SHETLAND SHIPPING CO., LTD. Aberdeen. First word: St. Leith, Aberdeen to Orkney and Shetland.

4. LIVERPOOL AND NORTH WALES S.S. CO., LTD. Liverpool. First word: St. Liverpool to Llandudno and Anglesey.

5. NEW MEDWAY STEAM PACKET CO., LTD. Rochester. Mostly *Queens*. South-east coast passenger excursion steamers.

6. BRITISH TRANSPORT COMMISSION (British Railways, Southern Region). London. Various names. Passenger, cargo and general services between British ports and British and Continental ports. Train and car ferries to the Continent. Excursion steamers.

7. BRITISH TRANSPORT COMMISSION (British Railways, Scottish Region); CALEDONIAN STEAM PACKET CO., LTD. Scottish place names, *Duchess of —, Maid of —*. Extensive ferry and passenger services in Clyde estuary. Summer excursions. Loch Lomond (*Maid of the Loch*).

8. COSENS & CO., LTD. Weymouth. Royal titles. Passenger excursion paddle steamers. Weymouth to Torquay, Bournemouth, Southampton and Isle of Wight.

9. DAVID MACBRAYNE, LTD. Glasgow. Prefix: *Loch*, with few exceptions. Passenger and cargo services between Clyde and Hebrides.

10. DUNDEE, PERTH AND LONDON SHIPPING CO., LTD. Dundee. Place names. London to English and Scottish East Coast ports.

11. BRITISH AND IRISH STEAM PACKET CO., LTD. Dublin. Irish place-names. Dublin to London, Southampton, Manchester, Bristol and Liverpool. Passenger, cargo and livestock.

12. SOUTHAMPTON, ISLE OF WIGHT AND SOUTH OF ENGLAND ROYAL MAIL STEAM PACKET CO., LTD. (Red Funnel Steamers, Ltd.). Southampton. Royal titles. Excursion steamers.

13. ISLE OF MAN STEAM PACKET CO., LTD. Douglas. Manx names. Isle of Man to Fleetwood, Ardrossan, Heysham, Dublin, Belfast.

14. CENTRAL ELECTRICITY AUTHORITY. Misc. names. *Poole —, Sir —, Pompey —*. Carry coal to power stations.

15. BURNS AND LAIRD LINES, LTD. London. Prefix: *Lairds*. Glasgow, and West Scottish ports, Northern Ireland and Eire.

16. P. & A. CAMPBELL, LTD. Bristol. Various names. Bristol Channel and South Coast excursion steamers.

17. THOMAS J. METCALF (Metcalf Motor Coasters). Christian name followed by *M*. Coasters and coastal tankers.

18. BELFAST STEAM SHIP CO., LTD. Belfast. First word: *Ulster*. Belfast and Londonderry to Manchester and Liverpool with passengers, cargo and livestock.

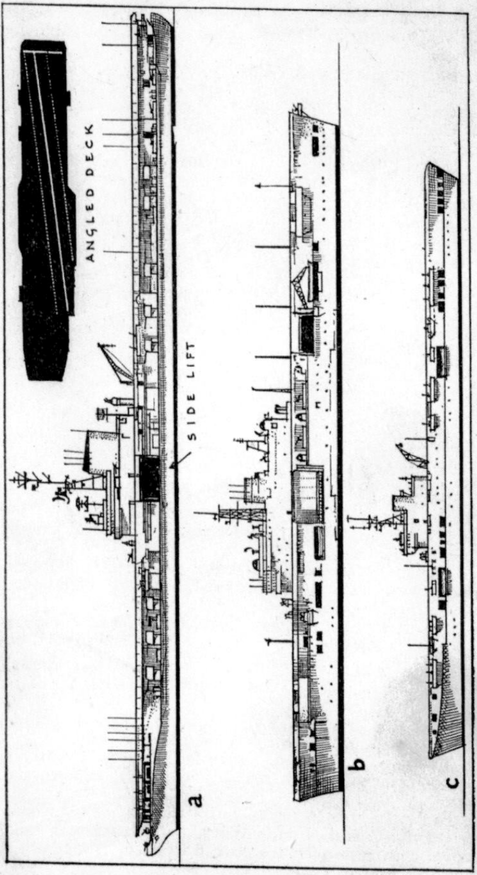

ANGLED DECK

SIDE LIFT

a

b

c

FIG. 35.—Aircraft carriers

AIRCRAFT CARRIER

(Plate XV)

THE aircraft carrier is easily recognized by the immense flight deck, with neither camber nor sheer, which stretches the full length and width of the vessel. The funnel, control tower, and navigating bridge form a narrow island superstructure on the starboard side. The carrier has no offensive guns but has a number of dual-purpose 4·5-in. or 5-in. guns and numerous light A.A. guns for self-defence. She has great endurance and a speed of 25 to 30 knots and, compared with the now obsolete battleship, only light armour. The deck may be of three-inch plating and the midships part of the hull strengthened by armour plating to protect the machinery.

A recent British invention sets the flight line between 5° and 8° from centre (see Fig. 35), thus an aircraft likely to overshoot can safely do so and make another touch down instead of flying into a crash barrier. Another British invention, the steam catapult, has also been fitted to R.N. and United States carriers to assist take off; rocket assistance is given on some vessels. The side aircraft lift and non-skid decks are other recent innovations. New developments are necessitated by the use of faster and heavier jet aircraft and the growth of guided missiles.

The largest carriers in the world are those of the U.S. *Forrestal* class with a load displacement of 75,900 tons, a length of 1,036 ft. o.a., and a speed of 35 knots. An 85,000-ton nuclear-powered aircraft carrier is already planned for the U.S. Navy.

Illustrations (Fig. 35)

(a) United States *Midway* class: 45,000 tons. 968 ft. o.a. 136 ft. deck width. 33 knots. Armament: 14—5-in. 40—3-in. 137 aircraft. Built 1945/47.

(b) British *Ark Royal*: 1955. 36,800 tons. 808 ft. o.a. 31·5 knots. 50–100 aircraft. Armament: 16—4·5-in. 34—40-mm. Bofors A.A.

(c) British *Glory* class: 1945/46. 13,190 tons. 695 ft. o.a. Flight deck 690 ft. by 80 ft. 25 knots. Armament: 29—40-mm. Bofors. 35 aircraft.

Similar carriers are owned by Netherlands, France, Canada, and Australia. The British *Hermes* class is intermediate between (b) and (c).

ARMAMENT OF BRITISH WARSHIPS

Calibre	Mounting, type, etc.	Type of warship
15-in.	Twin mounting in heavily armoured turrets.	Battleship *Vanguard* only, *King George V* class had 14-in.
6-in.	Twin or triple mounting in armoured turrets. Recent guns fully automatic. Dual purpose high and low angle.	9,000-ton cruisers—main armament.
5·25-in.	Twin mounting in armoured turrets.	Secondary armament of *Vanguard*. Main armament of 6,000-ton cruisers.
4·7-in.	Single or twin mounting in lightly armoured gunhouses or shields; splinter proof only.	Main armament of some destroyers.
4·5-in.	Single or twin mounting in lightly armoured gunhouses or shields.	Fleet carrier, main armament. Main armament of fleet escorts, destroyers and fast patrol gunboats.
4-in. and 4-in. A.A.	Single or twin mounting.	Secondary armament of 9,000-ton cruisers. Main armament of fast mine-layers, fleet anti-submarine frigates, some destroyers, most frigates. Main surface armament of a few submarines. Ocean minesweepers.
3-in.	Single mounting.	Secondary armament of *Tiger*-class cruisers. Main surface armament of some submarines.
Anti-aircraft guns 2-pdr. pompoms	Open or light shield. Multiple pompoms, eight barrels.	Most types of carrier and cruiser.
40-mm. Bofors	Mountings of one, two or six barrels. Open or light shields.	Main armament of light carriers. Secondary armament of fleet carriers. Main armament of coastal minesweepers, seaward defence boats. A.A. for most types of ship.
20-mm. Oerlikon	Single mountings, open or light shields. —	A.A. for most types of ship.
Heavy Machine-gun	—	Secondary surface armament of submarines. Main armament of motor mine-sweepers and some fast patrol boats.
21-in. torpedo tubes	Single mounts. Triple mounts. Quadruple mounts. Quintuple mounts.	Torpedo boats. Cruisers. Cruisers, destroyers. Fleet escorts and destroyers.
18-in. torpedo tubes	Single mounts.	Torpedo boats.
Guided missile Seaslug, ship-to-air missile	Triple-ramp launcher. Propelled by sustainer motor and four boosters. Fed automatically from magazine. Target detected by radar.	To be fitted to four new guided missile Fleet escorts. Experiments on guided-missile ship *Girdle Ness*.

BATTLESHIP

Just over fifty years ago the famous *Dreadnought* revolutionized the design of the battleship and set the pattern for the most important units of the world's navies. Heavily armoured and equipped with up to ten guns of 14- or 16-in. calibre, these battleships have dominated sea power for half a century. Now, however, the battleship's days are over and, with the development of the fast jet aircraft and guided missile replacing the big gun, the aircraft carrier has taken its place as the largest and most effective unit of a fleet.

In 1957 the Admiralty decided to scrap the four *King George V* class battleships which were built towards the end of the last war. The slightly larger *Vanguard* remains the sole British ship of this type.

The United States still possesses the *Iowa* and other battleships in reserve.

The future of the French *Jean Bart* and *Richelieu* and the American battleships is still undecided. The silhouette of the battleship cannot be mistaken for any other ship. Her huge size and great superstructure are easily identified and with the drastic reduction in numbers the few remaining ships are easily recognized as individual ships.

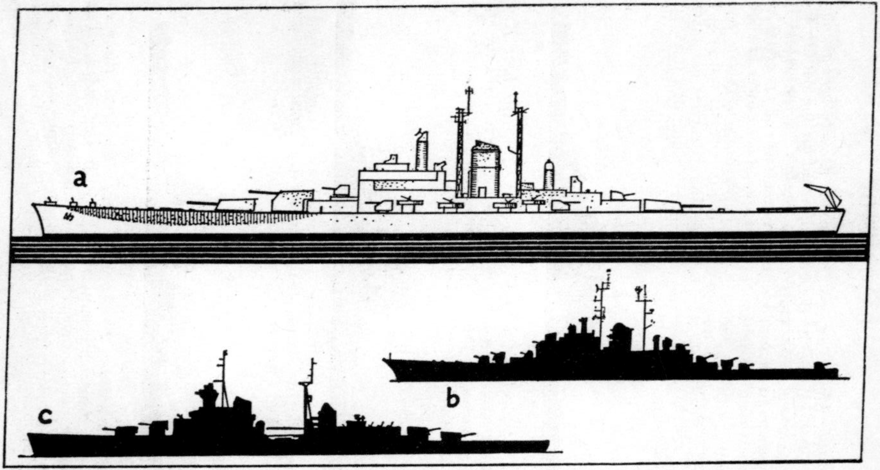

FIG. 36.—Cruisers—(I)

CRUISER—(I)

THE cruiser is a general-purpose fighting vessel designed for speed and endurance with a comparatively heavy armament. Endurance is particularly important to British and American cruisers in order to protect long trade routes all over the world. Other nations with different commitments are able to pay more attention to speed.

Cruisers vary in size from the large United States heavy cruisers of the *Des Moines* class with their nine 8-in. guns, to the British *Daring* class escorts which resemble small cruisers and take their duties.

The Royal Navy no longer possesses any 8-in. gun cruisers. The *Cumberland* is the sole survivor of the *County* class and she is now used as a trials cruiser.

The German pocket battleship (motor ship) was a hybrid type of warship with the displacement of a heavy cruiser—limited by treaty—but with 11-in. and 5·9-in. guns, giving a firing power more like that of a battleship. The armour of these ships was like that of the cruiser. They were designed mainly for commerce raiding.

Illustrations (Fig. 36)

(a) United States *Des Moines* class heavy cruiser: 1948/49. 17,000 tons. 716 ft. o.a. 33 knots 9—8-in. guns in triple turrets. 12—5-in. Numerous light A.A. guns. Armoured sides: 8 in. to 6 in., 2-in. decks.

(b) French *Colbert* class Anti-Aircraft cruiser: 1955. 8,500 tons. 597 ft. o.a. 32 knots. 16—5-in. A.A. guns. 24 Bofors A.A. guns. Later to have guided-missile armament.

(c) Russian *Sverdlov* class: 1950 onwards. 12,800 tons. 689 ft. o.a. 34·5 knots. 12—6-in. guns in triple turrets. 32—37-mm. A.A. guns. 10—21-in. tubes in quintuple mounting. 4-in. hull armour. The Russians possess some 1940/45 cruisers, smaller than the above, but fitted with 9—7·1-in. guns.

COLOURS OF SHIPPING COMPANIES

BRITISH COASTAL AND CONTINENTAL CARGO AND PASSENGER SERVICES—(II)

(*See* Plate XVII)

1. FRANK T. EVERARD & SONS, LTD. London. Words ending in *ity*. Coastwise services between British and Continental ports. Tugs and sailing barges.

2. BRITISH AND CONTINENTAL STEAMSHIP CO., LTD. Liverpool. Some bird names.

3. THE GENERAL STEAM NAVIGATION CO., LTD. London. Bird names. Coast and Continental services. Excursion steamers. Some buff funnels.

4. JOHN S. MONKS, LTD. Liverpool. Personal names and suffix: *ville*. Coastal services.

5. COAST LINES, LTD. Liverpool. Second word: *Coast*. Between most British ports. Some coastal passenger services. Associated with eight other coastwise shipping companies.

6. CURRIE LINE, LTD. Leith. Mostly place-names ending in *land*. Leith, Glasgow, Dundee, Liverpool, and Middlesbrough to Continent and Mediterranean.

7. WM. CORY & SONS, LTD. Newcastle-on-Tyne. Prefix: *Cor*. Coastwise services. Tankers.

8. WILLIAM ROBERTSON, SHIPOWNERS, LTD. Glasgow. Minerals and semi-precious stones. Tramping.

9. CONSTANTINE LINES, LTD. Middlesbrough. Suffix: *wood*. Colliers. Short sea trading. Mediterranean. General tramping.

10. MACANDREWS & CO., LTD. London. Spanish names. London, Glasgow and Liverpool.

11. WM. FRANCE, FENWICK & CO., LTD. London. Suffix: *wood*. Colliers and tramps.

12. TYNE-TEES STEAM SHIPPING CO., LTD. Newcastle-on-Tyne. Misc. names. Newcastle to London and Continent.

13. JOHN KELLY, LTD. Belfast. Prefix: *Bally*. Coastwise tramping.

14. HENRY AND MACGREGOR, LTD. Leith. Second word: *Head*. Coastwise tramping.

15. HUGHES HOLDEN SHIPPING, LTD. Liverpool. Second word: *Rose*. Coastwise tramping United Kingdom and Continent.

16. MOSS HUTCHISON LINE, LTD. Glasgow. Misc. names. United Kingdom to France, Spain, Portugal, Mediterranean and Black Sea. Some white hulls.

17. STEPHENSON CLARKE AND ASSOCIATED COMPANIES, LTD. London. Misc. names. Colliers carrying coal to power stations and gas works. Up-river colliers. Silver band on funnel.

18. COMBEN LONGSTAFF & CO., LTD., (Williamstown Shipping Co., Ltd.). London. Suffix: *brook*. Coastwise collier services.

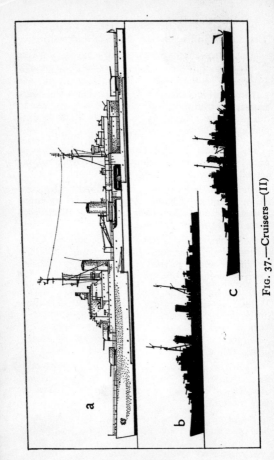

a

b

c

FIG. 37.—Cruisers—(II)

CRUISER—(II)

(Plate XVIII)

GREAT Britain, United States, France, and Russia all possess a number of cruisers with a main armament of 6-in. guns. With its all-purpose armament—including torpedo tubes—the light cruiser is a valuable ship for offensive and escort duties. The armour is generally limited to 4-in. plating at the sides protecting the engine room and 2-in. turret and deck protection. The latest British cruisers of the *Tiger* class are traditional ships, but the new *County* class will be armed with guided weapons.

The cruiser silhouette varies a good deal. The arrangement and shape of the funnels vary more than any other type of warship. British cruisers often have the forward funnel placed at a higher level than the after funnel and whereas the United States ships are flush-decked, British, French, and Russian cruisers usually have a long forecastle. In common with other warships of to-day cruisers are growing more and more antennae as new electronic equipment is brought into use.

Illustrations (Fig. 37)

(a) British *Superb* class cruiser: 1944/45. 9,000 tons. 555 ft. o.a. 29 knots. 9—6-in. guns. 10—4-in. 6—21-in. torpedo tubes.

(b) British *Dido* class cruiser: 1940/44. 6,000 tons. 512 ft. o.a. 32 knots. 8 or 10—5.25-in. guns in twin turrets. 6—21-in. torpedo tubes in triple mounts.

(c) United States *Cleveland* class cruiser: 1942/45. 10,000 tons. 610 ft. o.a. 33 knots. 12—6-in. guns in triple mounts. 12—5-in. guns in twin mounts. Now in reserve.

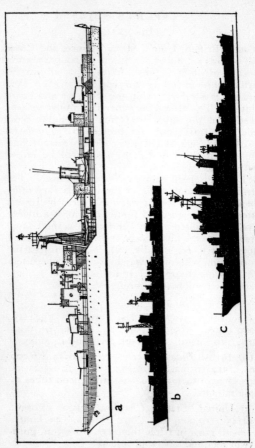

FIG. 38.—Fleet escorts

FLEET ESCORTS

(Plate XIX)

BEFORE the last war France possessed a large number of "super" destroyers of 3,000 tons displacement, considerable armament and speeds of over 40 knots. These *contre-torpilleurs* were by far the fastest destroyers of the period. The new *Surcouf* class ships are similar but not quite so fast. The German war-time *Narvik* class destroyers were also large destroyers with 5·9-in. guns in armoured turrets; some of these vessels are now owned by France and Russia. The British post-war *Daring* class ships—no longer designated as destroyers—are warships designed to do duty as fleet escorts or light reconnaissance cruisers. They are fitted with the latest anti-submarine and anti-aircraft equipment and radar controlled fully automatic 4·5-in. guns in twin turrets. Individual ships vary a little in silhouette, particularly with regard to the after funnel. The forward funnel is a sloping, curved type almost hidden by the lattice mast.

The *Weapon* class Fleet anti-submarine escorts (*see* page 75) are similar in appearance to the *Daring* class, but they have fewer and smaller guns.

Illustrations (Fig. 38)

(a) British *Daring* class: 1952/54. 2,610 tons. 390 ft. o.a. 30 knots. 6—4·5-in. guns in twin turrets. 6—40-mm. A.A. 10—21-in. tubes. A/S squid.

(b) French *Surcouf* class: 1954. 2,750 tons. 422 ft. o.a. 34 knots. 6—5-in. A.A. guns. 6—20-mm. A.A. 6—2·25-in. A.A. 12—21·7-in. tubes.

(c) United States *Mitscher* class (classed as frigate): 1953/4. 3,675 tons. 493 ft. o.a. 35 knots. 2—5-in. 4—3-in. 4—21-in. tubes. 2 rocket projectors.

FIG. 39.—Destroyers

DESTROYER

THE destroyer is a small warship with a comparatively shallow draught and she is therefore able to visit many small ports and will be more familiar than the larger warships. She is designed for high speed and good manœuvrability. She has an all-purpose armament but no armour plating; her best defence is her speed and flexibility of movement. The destroyer may have conventional guns, light anti-aircraft weapons, depth charge throwers, torpedoes, or guided missiles. The *Battle* class destroyer has the typical British silhouette with a single funnel and long forecastle deck. Most American destroyers have two funnels.

Apart from general duties some destroyers are equipped for specific work as radar pickets, anti-submarine activities, or mine-laying.

The flotilla leader is a destroyer fitted to serve as the administrative headquarters ship for the flotilla; she is distinguished by a black band round the top of the forward funnel or the foremost visible funnel.

Illustrations (Fig. 39)

(a) Canadian *Tribal* class: 1942/48. 2,000 tons. 377 ft. o.a. 32 knots. 4—4-in. guns. 2—3-in. 4—40-mm. A.A. 4—21-in. tubes. These ships are now fitted with lattice masts and the three Australian *Tribals* are equipped as anti-submarine destroyers.

(b) British *Battle* class: 1946/47. 2,460 tons. 379 ft. o.a. 4—4.5-in. guns. 8—40-mm. A.A. 10—21-in. tubes. 30 knots. The main armament is all placed forward.

(c) United States *Gleaves* class: 1940/43. 1,600 tons. 348 ft. o.a. 33 knots. 4—5-in. guns. 4—40-mm. A.A. 5—21-in. tubes. This vessel represents a large group built during the war. The modern American destroyers are larger but similarly armed and are capable of the same speed. They have more up-to-date electronic equipment.

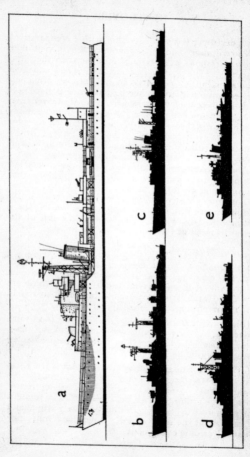

a

b

c

d

e

FIG. 40.—Frigates

FRIGATE

(Plate XXII)

THE term "frigate" is now used for a wide variety of ships with a tonnage ranging from 1,000 to 2,000 tons and a range of speed from about 15 knots up to that of a destroyer. The frigate has no standard armament but is primarily used for anti-submarine duty and the escort of merchant vessels. The term is even more confusing with the United States present use of "frigate" for a vessel which at one time would have been classed as a light cruiser. British frigates included ships built as such, converted fleet destroyers, converted escort destroyers and many other types of small vessels. Modern motor frigates are designed as anti-aircraft ships for the protection of convoys. The dividing line between the fast frigate and the destroyer is almost impossible to define.

Illustrations (Fig. 40)

(a) Fast anti-submarine frigate "T" class: 1,170 tons. 362 ft. o.a. 31·25 knots. 2—4-in. guns in a twin mount and 7—40-mm. Bofors guns in single and twin mounts. Two anti-submarine depth-charge throwers—squids. This type of frigate is a limited conversion from a fleet destroyer.

(b) *Leopard* class anti-aircraft frigate: 1,738 tons. 340 ft. o.a. 21 knots. 4—4·5-in. guns in twin mounts and 2—40-mm. Bofors guns. 8 squids. This is a new type of frigate for convoy escort or duty as a destroyer for offensive action. The *Leopard* class is unusual in that it is propelled by diesel engines.

(c) "R" class anti-submarine frigate: 1,705 tons fully loaded. 358 ft. o.a. 31·25 knots. 2—4-in. guns in a twin mount with 2—40-mm. Bofors A.A. guns. This class is fully converted from former fleet destroyers. The "U", "V", and "W" class are similar in appearance and performance. Many other destroyers are being similarly converted.

(d) *Bay* class frigate: 1,580 tons fully loaded. 307 ft. o.a. 4—4-in. guns. 6—40-mm., 2—20-mm. A.A. Depth-charge throwers. Numerous frigates of this class and the similar *Loch* and *River* classes were built between 1940 and 1945. They have a speed of 19 knots.

(e) *Hunt* class anti-aircraft frigates: 1,175 tons fully loaded. *c.* 280 ft. o.a. Speed 24–29 knots. 4/6—4-in. guns. 2-pdr. pompoms and 20-mm. A.A. The numerous vessels in this class are converted from the war-time *Hunt* class escort destroyers.

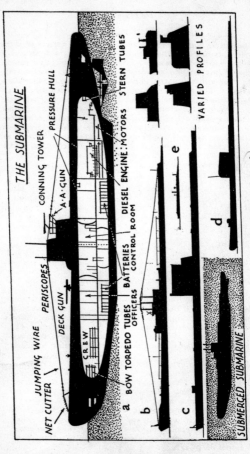

THE SUBMARINE

JUMPING WIRE
NET CUTTER
PERISCOPES
DECK GUN
CONNING TOWER
PRESSURE HULL
A·A·GUN
STERN TUBES
DIESEL ENGINE · MOTORS
CONTROL ROOM
BATTERIES
OFFICERS
BOW TORPEDO TUBES
CREW

a

b

c

d

e

VARIED PROFILES

SUBMERGED SUBMARINE

FIG. 41.—Details of the submarine

SUBMARINE

THE essential feature of the submarine is the long cigar-shaped pressure hull which contains all the machinery and living quarters. On each side of this hull is a blister hull containing ballast tanks. The small superstructure amidships is the bridge and conning tower, within which is the main hatch giving access to the hull. Two periscopes lead up from the control room. The present tendency is to stream the superstructure and increase its height so that the periscope standards do not project. United States conning towers are usually placed well forward of amidships. Forward or abaft the conning tower is a platform for a light A.A. gun, and on the other side at deck level is a gun of about 4-in. calibre. Sometimes two deck guns are carried.

The torpedo tubes are fitted in the bows and stern. Two forms of propulsion are used: diesel engines when surfaced and electric motors when submerged. In U.S.A. the first nuclear-propelled submarine was launched in 1954 with a projected range of 30,000 miles and a speed of 25 knots. The projected British submarine *Dreadnought* is to be propelled by atomic power. Submarine designers are constantly concerned with increasing both the underwater speed and underwater range.

The "snort" is an innovation which enables the vessel to take in fresh air while she is travelling at periscope level. A British submarine has now made a 2,500-mile Atlantic crossing without surfacing.

Illustrations (Fig. 41)

(b) British "A" class Submarine: 1945/48. 1,120 tons standard. 281 ft. o.a. 18 knots surface and 8 knots submerged. Some vessels have one 4-in. gun. Machine-guns. 10—21-in. tubes. Superstructure of this class is being modernized.

(c) British *Porpoise* class: 1956. c. 1,500 tons standard, 295 ft. o.a.

(d) British *Explorer* class: 1954. 780 tons. 225 ft. o.a. 24/25 knots underwater. An experimental type with new type of propulsion using diesel oil in decomposed hydrogen peroxide. Fast underwater speed. Latest equipment.

(e) British "X" class midget submarine: c. 30 tons. 54 ft. o.a. Diesels and electric motors. Speed about 6 knots submerged. Crew of five.

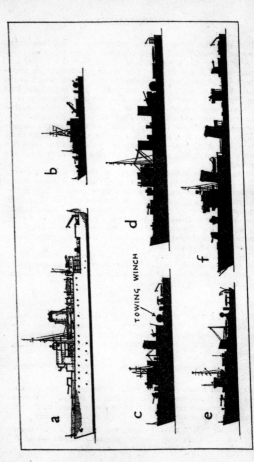

Fig. 42.—Minesweepers

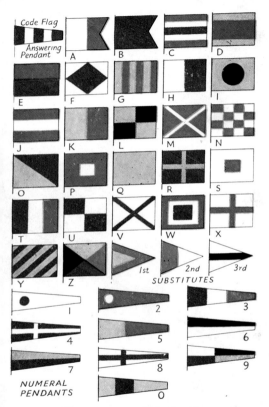

PLATE I.—International Code flags (*see* p. 20)

PLATE II.—Passenger and mail liner Cunard R.M.S. *Caronia* (34,183 tons) and an American tug

Courtesy of British Transport Commission

PLATE III

Upper: Blue Funnel cargo and passenger liner *Jason* 10,160 g.t. (*see* p. 39)

Lower: British Railways passenger and car ferry *Lord Warden* 3,333 g.t. on the Dover–Boulogne route (*see* pp. 51 and 55)

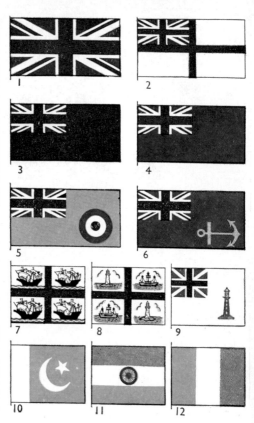

PLATE IV.—National flags and ensigns (I)
(*see* p. 28)